THE EPISCOPAL CHURCH AND EDUCATION

The Episcopal Church and Education

Edited by

KENDIG BRUBAKER CULLY

MOREHOUSE-BARLOW CO.
New York

The Scripture quotations in this book marked "RSV" are from the Revised Standard Version of *The Holy Bible,* copyrighted 1946, 1952, and 1957 by the Division of Christian Education, National Council of the Churches of Christ in the United States of America.

CONTRIBUTORS

STEPHEN FIELDING BAYNE, JR., S.T.D., D.D., LL.D., LITT.D., L.H.D.
Bishop, Vice President, The Executive Council of the Protestant Episcopal Church

LEE A. BELFORD, PH.D.
Chairman, Department of Religious Education, New York University

MYRON B. BLOY, JR., M.A.
Executive Director, Church Society for College Work

ALLEN F. BRAY III
Chaplain, Culver Military Academy

WOOD B. CARPER, JR., D.D.
Professor of Pastoral Theology, The General Theological Seminary

DORA P. CHAPLIN, S.T.D.
Professor of Christian Education, The General Theological Seminary

KENDIG BRUBAKER CULLY, PH.D.
Dean, New York Theological Seminary

JOHN MAURICE GESSELL, PH.D.
Administrative Assistant to the Dean, School of Theology, University of the South

CARMAN ST. JOHN HUNTER, L.H.D.
Executive Secretary, Department of Christian Education, The Executive Council of the Protestant Episcopal Church

ALDEN D. KELLEY, S.T.D., D.D.
Professor of Theology and Philosophy of Religion, Bexley Hall, Kenyon College

REAMER KLINE, D.D.
President, Bard College

RANDOLPH CRUMP MILLER, PH.D., S.T.D., D.D.
Horace Bushnell Professor of Christian Nurture, Yale University

MAX M. PEARSE, JR., REL.ED.D.
Professor of Christian Education, Church Divinity School of the Pacific

5

H. BOONE PORTER, JR., PH.D.
Professor of Liturgics, The General Theological Seminary
JOHN T. RUSSELL
Rector, Christ the King Episcopal Church, Orlando, Florida

PREFACE

EDUCATION is a process and a function belonging to the entire society, just as the Christian religion must certainly be said to pertain to the whole Body of Christ. It would be impossible and inappropriate to make any claim that the *total* educational task related to any one segment of society (family, or school, or even the state), just as it would be the height of foolishness (if not only of pride) to insist that any one of the broken parts of the universal Church possessed a monopoly on Christian truth or experience.

Yet the educational process is always carried out not in general but through particular manifestations of the society, whether geographically, spatially, or otherwise conditioned. And the people of God must make their profession of faith and their public witness in and through a particular segment of the one Body of Christ. The interrelationship of the institutions of society concerned with education are apparent, in spite of the particularized form in which any given educational thrust shows itself. Likewise, any one denomination of the whole Church of Christ certainly cannot operate in a vacuum, since much of its vitality and many of its formulations will necessarily coincide with or parallel similar forms and actions to be found in neighboring communions.

Sometimes the Christian religion and education coalesce, as they must necessarily do since education cannot be completely divorced from the religious impulses of people, any more than the Church could hope to flourish unless it reached educationally into the society about. Thus it is obvious that the particular educational expressions of the religious community can never be considered in any absolute separateness.

However, it would appear to be good at this juncture of time to have every denomination's educational history, impulses, practices, and intentions examined rather intensively in order that what is distinctive or of special interest to it may be presented both to its own people and to the entire Christian community, as well as to the "secular" society.

As far as one knows, this is the first reasonably comprehensive effort to look at a wide spectrum of educational questions through the perspective of the Episcopal Church. The scope of this book extends from the local parish to the national church, from peculiarly denominational involvements to confrontation not only with other Christian bodies but with other world religions as well. These are individual interpretations of scholars who write out of their own understandings of the material with which they deal. Neither individual writers nor the whole group of writers would presume to suggest that they are offering any "official" word about the Episcopal Church and education. It is hoped, however, that from these perspectives will emerge a kind of panoramic view, at least, of the kinds of involvements and concerns Episcopalians have had in the past and have in the present with regard to education, broadly conceived. Perchance there might even be plausible hints as to likely patterns of emergent developments.

KENDIG BRUBAKER CULLY

New York City
Epiphany, 1966

CONTENTS

9

PART I
The Parish Level

1

THE SUNDAY
CHURCH SCHOOL:
HERITAGE AND
PROSPECT

BY *John Maurice Gessell*

M OSES Herzog, Saul Bellow's non-hero, shared the
American intellectual's alienation from the world. This
very sense of isolation afforded him, however, a sharpened
focus on fuzzy realities. Herzog was keenly aware of the unfolding meaning of his own life. "The question of ordinary
human experience," he wrote, "is the principal question of
these modern centuries, as Montaigne and Pascal, otherwise
in disagreement, both clearly saw . . . the strength of a
man's virtue or spiritual capacity measured by his ordinary
life." [1] Now this is a decisively qualified perspective on the
meaning of experience in the world. All perspectives have
their particular qualifications—this is what makes them ways
of looking—but this one is clearer than many and consciously
held.

Herzog was no secularist, but he was what R. Gregor
Smith has called "the new man." Herzog would have taken
seriously Bonhoeffer's warning to religious people: ". . . our

13

coming of age forces us to a true recognition of our situation *vis-à-vis* God. God is teaching us that we must live as man who can get along very well without him. . . . The God who makes us live in this world without using him as a working hypothesis is the God before whom we are ever standing." [2]

We see this when Herzog's future wife, reflecting on her experience, told him that she had had a terrible childhood. "My parents damn near destroyed me," she said. "All right— it doesn't matter . . . I believe in my Saviour, Jesus Christ. I'm not afraid of death . . . But don't expect me to go along the ordinary loose way—without rules. No! It'll be these rules or nothing." Herzog could not accept this way of escape for himself and he wrote an imaginary letter to his wife's priest. "I thought it might interest you to learn the true history of one of your converts, Monsignor," he thought, and then continued by musing about the priest himself. "Ecclesiastical dolls—gold-threaded petticoats, whining organ pipes. The actual world, to say nothing of the infinite universe, demanded a sterner, a real masculine character." [3]

With unerring accuracy the artist shatters our illusions and pretensions, especially those that Christians have about themselves. We produce ecclesiastical dolls who live in a prison house of rules, and reduce God to a control device for our comfort. A doll cannot live in the world in any other way. The God of the Bible is trusted, if at all, as an escape hatch.

The Sunday Church school participates in and confounds this *grotesquerie*. The history of the Sunday school bears this out. When effective it is seized upon as an instrument of propaganda. When out of fashion it becomes fashionable to scorn or ignore it. Generally committed to various forms of propositional teaching and information-giving, its prospects depend on how we will choose to deal with this religious and educational distortion now. Does the Church—do we?—really wish to create an effective instrument for genuine religious education? John Heuss once wrote that the "demands of the new curriculum are what make it significant, and what scare people off," and Randolph Crump Miller identified this as the "demand of the Gospel" which we fear.[4]

Behind this question lies a fundamental religious consideration implying the necessity for decision. Is the world a dynamic, open, unfolding, surprising place where God's call is to a pilgrimage of obedient, responsive love undertaken with risk? Or is it a static place, closed, completed, predictable, where God's call is understood as obedience to some concept of truth?

In the former case the curriculum for Christian education will be a design for the guiding and deepening of Christian experience toward the enhancement of people's capacities to respond faithfully *to* the call of God without a guarantee. In the latter case the curriculum for Christian education will be a design for learning the once-for-all given truths *about* God. The former seeks to help people find their lives in an ambiguous world where God's self-disclosure is never the revelation of final truth or fixed rules which guarantee safety. The latter seeks conformity to a body of knowledge and submission to its truth as final, giving the believer the illusion of control. The former seeks the maturity of the learner, the latter his indoctrination.

This contrast between two views of the world and of curriculum is no doubt exaggerated, but its purpose is to dramatize the issue which we confront in any consideration of the future of the Sunday Church school. Will it be ecclesiastical dolls, or faith in the living God who will not let us use him as a working hypothesis? There is an ineluctable difference between the dynamic and the static, classical view. The classical Christian view was of the world well furnished with the furniture in its proper place. It only lacked that we learn the places, acknowledge its order and arrangement, and never transgress the limits. This view of the world, together with its inadequate metaphysical and theological assumptions, is simply untenable in a post-Kantian world. The history of the Sunday Church school is the history of the resulting curriculum conflicts.

Resistance to Educational Theory

Beginning as charity schools to teach underprivileged children to read and write, the Sunday schools were freed by the spread of general public education to engage in religious instruction. Their education models, inherited from the Reformation and the 18th century, were moralistic and catechetical. One of the astonishing results of a review of the history of the Sunday school is to note its remarkable resistance to educational theory. While new developments occurred throughout the nineteenth century in the field of general education, Church leaders called for catechetical instruction as the norm for Sunday school teaching.

While the history of the Sunday Church school cannot be told here, it is possible to note some major turning points in its development. The Episcopal Sunday school became a conscious instrument for religious education with the organization in 1826 of the General Protestant Episcopal Sunday School Union. Its recommended scheme of operation was catechetical and propositional. But the rise of the early Sunday religious schools had all of the success and enthusiasm of what we would call a "movement." Less emphasis was placed on disciplined institutional structure than on its evangelical impulse, at first to reach the poor and, in some parts of the country, "people of color," and then all children of the Church. The G.P.E.S.S.U. in its reports from 1826 to

1832 emphasized the Church's "duty assiduously to instruct her younger members in the nature of her own peculiar character . . . [and] the principles of Christianity in [sic] its purest form . . ." [5]

As is true of a movement, the growth of Sunday schools was rapid, and they were essentially dependent on lay leadership. At one time, St. George's Church in New York City alone had six schools, although there was characteristically a strong undenominational flavor about the movement. At first the Sunday school movement appears to have been associated with the early evangelicals, displaying characteristic concerns to reach all people, to teach the Bible, and to engage in uplift and moral reform.

Like many movements, the Sunday school met with early success and its initial enthusiasm made it an uncommonly effective educational instrument. It did not, however, develop a professional literature or professionally trained leaders. Within a decade of the founding of the G.P.E.S.S.U., both a lowering of the prescribed standards of the Union's scheme of operation and gathering criticism brought this early period of development to an end.

Already discernible at the Union's founding is the suborning of the Sunday school to the purposes of propaganda and recruitment. From that time to this, controversies over curriculum and educational method have marked the Church's inability to decide whether it wants an educational or an indoctrinational program. In its *Circular* of 1826 the Union called on the Church so to instruct her younger members

> that they might at all times be ready to state the grounds of their attachment to her pale, and thus be armed against any temptations to dereliction from her faith and discipline. . . . Sunday Schools under the patronage of the Protestant Episcopal Church should be conducted on principles purely Prot-

estant Episcopalian, and should afford a prominent place in their instruction to the doctrines and constitution of the Church to which they belong.

In the meantime the tradition of catechetical instruction had continued, both within and outside of the Sunday school movement. By 1835 the once promising movement appeared to have lost its early effectiveness. Its undenominational nature and its lay character made some Church leaders view it with disfavor. Men like Doane and Hobart strongly advocated catechization as the normal and canonical mode of education, thus continuing to fasten on the Church a rote system of instruction.

At the same time, the responsibility for Sunday school education was passing from the evangelicals to the high-church party. The Sunday school movement was in fact caught up in the churchmanship split following 1844, and the Sunday School Union, captured by the tractarians, continued to decline in importance.[6] Parallel to this were the indifference and hostility of many clergy. The Joint Commission of the General Convention of 1835 followed this retrograde movement. In 1841 the commission, consciously influenced by the tractarian movement, echoed the call for catechetical instruction and, as a churchmanship issue, advocated parish day schools in the place of Sunday schools as the Church's normal means of religious instruction. The same call was reiterated in 1865 by General Convention's Committee on Christian Education, whose report belittled and condemned Sunday schools as "unchurchly." In succeeding conventions the committee very nearly ignored the Sunday school altogether.

Thus, from 1826 into the 1870's we see early achievement followed by dormancy, fostered in part by the control of an unfriendly interest.

The 1870's to the 1940's

Characteristically, the revival of the Sunday school in the 1870's came about at first for the familiar institutional reasons. While the Sunday School Union was expending its energies against the Evangelical Knowledge Society, it was noted that the religious instruction of children was languishing and especially along the frontier areas of the country. The American Church Sunday School Institute was formed during 1875-1884, predicated on a growing anxiety for the prevention of the loss of children to the Church, a concern echoed in the 1940's.

With the passing of the sharpness of the churchmanship controversy and a renewed concern with the Sunday school as a potential educational force, the long-orphaned institution was belatedly "adopted" by the Church. The General Convention of 1905 established a Joint Commission on Sunday School Instruction. This act was followed in 1913 by the General Board of Religious Education, and in 1919 by the National Council's Department of Religious Education.

In the meantime, a striking characteristic of the period of the Sunday school's revival—following 1870 and the earlier period of dormancy, derision, and neglect—was that modern educational theory began to inform the discussion.

While the new educational theories of Pestalozzi, advocating the method of education of children through their own activity, and the ensuing controversy with Herbartian indoctrinationalism went unnoticed during the early rise and development of the Sunday school movement, the characteristic approach of Church leaders to religious instruction, based on catechetical methods, was that of indoctrination. Revelation was held to be a set of truths about God, and the Bible was a book primarily for moral instruction. Memory and rote learning were used almost exclusively, as the literature for Sunday school instruction makes clear.[7] There was an almost studied neglect of sound educational advice. Henry F. Cope, an early leader in the Religious Education Association, complained that the uniform lessons for Sunday school use were developed despite the advice of trained educators.[8]

But the Religious Education Association, organized in 1903 under the leadership of William Rainey Harper, then President of the University of Chicago, instantly made its influence felt. Its aims included that of placing the educational work of the Church on a level with general education. Men such as George Albert Coe fostered new methods for religious instruction in line with the developments in educational theory of Francis Parker and John Dewey, who placed the child and his interests in the center of the educational process. This in turn led to more effective teaching methods. (The contemporary distortions of something called "progressive education" by both critics and practitioners have little relevance here.) Coe, among others, viewed education in its teleological significance, as an instrument for the discovery of the ultimate values on which people can base and interpret their lives. He and others took seriously the "laws of learning" based on the newly discovered developmental patterns of the living, growing human organism.

The force of the Religious Education Association made itself felt in the Episcopal Church. Its educational understandings and methods influenced the work of the Church's educational leaders. The period from 1904 through the 1930's was generally one of creative thought and planning for Sunday school instruction. The shift in understanding and interest was signaled by the report of the Joint Commission on Sunday School Instruction in 1907.

Pascal Harrower, writing in the June, 1910, issue of *Reli-*

gious Education, described the curriculum plan as reported by the Joint Commission. More than a "Bible school," the Sunday school was to afford the "largest possible knowledge of the principles of religion" on the basis of a graded curriculum worked out in accordance with the recognized laws of child development. A taste of this may be obtained by noting the stated aim of the primary department of the Sunday school: "To plant in the heart of the child those first truths of Christianity, which underlie the Lord's Prayer, the Creed and the Ten Commandments, viz., God's love, care, wisdom, power—which form the basis for inculcating obedience and love, and inspiring reverence and worship in the child."

This statement is curiously paralleled in some of the recent Seabury Series material. While it is naïve in its view and its methodological understanding of seeking to implant principles as a basis for Christian response, it is none the less a clear indication that professional religious education in the Episcopal Church had laid the catechetical and indoctrinational ghost.

Following this pre-World War I period came William E. Gardner and his theory of Christian nurture leading to the Christian Nurture Series of the 1920's and 1930's. Writing in *The Children's Challenge to the Church* (1914), Gardner said that religious education is not "a process of intellectualism . . . of conveying or announcing truth." Nurture is a matter of training the inner life and this no information can ever do. Religious education is "a life." [9]

Thus the period from 1875 to the 1930's, following its capture by the high-church party and its decline and dormancy, was one of revival and of new life in religious education in the Episcopal Church. For the greater part, the Sunday school, no longer the captive of a party, became the instrument for effective religious education, supported by competent professional educators and the concern of vast numbers of people.

However, the controversy over curriculum theory had not been resolved. The tension between experience-centered theories of nurture and indoctrinationalist views continued. It was not until the period of the 1940's and 1950's that the issue could be clearly joined. By that time the thrust and the vitality of the early decades of the twentieth century had lost their momentum and, indeed, had been outgrown. But the new crisis was, again, viewed as institutional and demographical. The accomplishments of those earlier decades were challenged in 1945 by the fact of the alarming loss of confirmed persons (the catch phrase in those days was "seven out of ten") and the suggested remedy of a "return to the teachings of the Church." A power struggle was developing in which the counters were opposing views of education which the Church has since been taught to call vulgarly the tension between "content" and "process." To this we now turn.

The "New" Curriculum

The complex history of this intriguing and tragic chapter in Church history has, for the most part, been told in an unpublished dissertation by Dorothy Braun.[10] While she has collected many of the facts, she has not, however, always been able to interpret their meaning. My care here will be simply to seek to make clear the nature of the disastrous outcome of the struggle.

Disaster was built in by the statement of the House of Bishops, meeting in 1945, calling for proper instruction in the essential teachings of the Church's discipline and doctrine. The understandings of the religious education movement were thereby challenged by a "content" and an indoctrinationalist view of the teaching-learning process as the answer to the Church's loss of hold over its people and growing indifference to its teachings. What pressures operated to attempt this departure from accepted educational procedure?

There were two discernible factors which, unless they are distinguished, lead to confusion. This is precisely what happened in the 1950's. First, the Church was facing a cultural and sociological crisis. The growing indifference in America to Christianity and its teachings, a secularist trend only in part delayed by the post-World War II re-examination of values, made its implications felt in the evident erosion of Christian faith and practice. The bishops saw this in terms of a loss of people and of growing indifference. They sounded the alarm as a crisis in the curriculum for religious education.

The second factor, and one largely independent of the sociological phenomenon, was an urgently recognized need to re-examine the presuppositions and basic principles of the curriculum for Christian education. Postponed by the war, this was a task which many realized should have been undertaken a decade earlier. Why were these two factors confused and placed into causal relation? Why was the crisis in allegiance, a long term secular trend with deep and complex roots, blamed on poor educational practices?

I suggest that in part this was due, given the perennial Protestant necessity to engage in curriculum revision as part of the ambiguity of our cultural situation, to the natural propensity to seek to assign blame when things go wrong. The Sunday school curriculum has always been fair game for those whose responsibility is the well-being of the Church. While the Church indeed shares in the responsibility for the secularist trend, to make the curriculum for Christian education the cause is both wrongheaded and unjust. People learn what they are ready to learn and act on values when they are ready to accept them. Their indifference is the cause, not the effect, of an inadequate educational system. Poor education does not create indifference and regardless of curriculum theory, people are less and less moved by the Church's claims, a social phenomenon which will not be immediately affected by curriculum revision.

Nevertheless, in 1945 a first-class brawl was shaping up between parties holding opposing views of curriculum at a time when the whole question of curriculum theory and design needed careful re-examination. Undoubtedly the power struggle obscured the fundamental issues, skewing them badly enough to make it questionable whether they can easily be re-appraised during this generation. Furthermore, I believe that the curriculum controversy of 1945-52 in the Episcopal Church is a frightening reflection of the Church's misunderstanding of Christianity in our day.

The bishops' anxiety, however, afforded a time for a significant and perhaps unexcelled development in curriculum theory for religious education. The irony is that the call for a "new curriculum" was essentially a regressive move, rooted in a misunderstanding of the Church and of education. But it was a move which, in the providence of God, opened the way for the articulation to the Church of an understanding of curriculum which was freshly innovative and a genuine contribution to curriculum theory. It was also clearly revolutionary and led to an explosion.

This built-in conflict eventually convulsed the Department of Christian Education. By the summer of 1952 the early architects of curriculum within the curriculum development division of the department were dismissed, and the production of undeniably handsome but educationally ambiguous materials became the focus of the department's operation. With this resolution of the power struggle, those who understand education basically as information-giving won the day.

But with a difference. Sophisticated educational theory could not be instantly dismissed and the professional staff could not, of course, settle for mere propositional teaching. Contemporary educational methods call for taking the person and his experience seriously in an attempt to find the relation between the Church's teaching and his own life. The result was the Seabury Series—now The Church's Teaching —a body of material to be imparted in some manner.

The Department of Christian Education, as a result of the call for a new curriculum, ended up with a new look on the old stuff. Christian education is by them understood as a process in which we begin with our knowledge of God's action and seek to uncover the needs in people to which this Gospel can be applied. The psychological hazards and the temptation to educational manipulation implicit in this view are manifest. The attempt to "meet people's needs" as the root of educational methodology is the betrayal of a naïve psychological orientation. It is not good education.

The details of the period 1945 to the present in the development of curriculum theory are too intricate to bear rehearsing here. It will be helpful to our purpose, however, to point out the innovative direction in which the curriculum department division, under the leadership of Vesper O. Ward, was proposing to move. Ward was familiar with contemporary educational developments and had long been aware that where the Church's educational program was ineffective, education was viewed as information-giving and indoctrination. He also knew that the curriculum issue needed re-examination.

Ward's approach was a basic reorientation of the definition of curriculum, not as materials nor as methods, but as life itself. The problem was not to produce materials about religion, but to use the dynamics of parish life so as to create the possibility for people to participate now in the ongoing drama of redemption. The curriculum, he believed, was a religious issue even more than an educational issue.

Dr. Ward began to work out some of these specific understandings in 1951-2 with the help of the late Charles F. Penniman, then director of the Educational Center in St. Louis. Together they sought to show that curriculum is basically the development of parish life and that materials would have to come out of the life of the parish rather than be imposed on the parish from an editor's office. The curriculum must deal with the fact that every person in his day-to-day living has to make sense out of what is naturally nonsense—the muddle of his own life—by knowing a God who is real for him. Hence the function of the curriculum for Christian education is to help all people find and understand their way among the mighty acts of God, done for us men and our salvation. The emphasis in this view (not novel, but articulated within the context of reputable educational theory and of theological exactness) was on human redemption through the dynamics of parish life and, in this process, on the development of educational resources related to these issues.[11]

This kind of talk clearly brought the whole Church under judgment, both as to the quality of its own life as expressed in the parishes, and in a Christian view of reality in which life by its own logic does not add up and must be radically redeemed. This has always been the biblical view but one which runs counter to the rather bland view of the static world in which education is conceived not as challenge but as correct information. Since these two challenges were not easy to live with, the conflict in the Department came out into the open. Penniman was asked to finish his work by the summer of 1952 and Ward left shortly thereafter.

Heritage and Prospects

What then has been the Sunday school's heritage? Certainly not institutional strength and sophistication. At times orphaned and ignored, at times seized for partisan advantage, the Church has not succeeded in building an enduring educational institution of viability and flexibility. Further, the Sunday school has inherited the results of the lack of accountability and responsibility of permanent professionally trained leadership. Unconcern, manipulation, and mismanagement have been accompanied by irrelevance and incompetence. As noted earlier, the single striking aspect of the history of religious education in America has been, until more recently, its innocence of educational competence. The Sunday school has generally been regarded, not as a serious educational undertaking where the concern for persons is paramount, but as a device for indoctrination and for fastening people into the institution, for recruitment and propaganda, institutional concerns which are incompatible with good education.

Beyond indifference, the Sunday school has also inherited in the Episcopal Church the still unresolved curriculum issue. But this may be positively appreciated. The accomplishments of Ward, Penniman, and others, though apparently of no determinative value to the final development of the new curriculum, have been the means of deepening insight and hope to many who are now enabled to see the true function of the Christian Church. Part of this achievement lay in the strengthening and deepening of the growing tradition of professional competence, and of the concern and devotion of many splendid lay teachers. The still unresolved curriculum issue continues to ferment. With this lies the hope of future prospects for the Sunday Church school as an effective instrument in the life and work of the Church.

It is our loss that the fundamental formulations of Ward and Penniman have not fully informed the present work of the Department, too easily persuaded to put gimmicks in the place of responsible educational methods. We currently observe the present confused and ill-informed training program, based on mechanical models, ineptly adapted from the growing body of human relations disciplines.

The prospects for the Sunday school appear in part to lie in the recovery and deepening of the work in curriculum begun in the early days of the present program. We see curriculum as a design for personal and social change. Ward has pointed out that it arises out of the dynamics of the religious life of the parish itself and, where learning is to go on, is that structured, guided, deepened, enriched, and expanded experience which affords people the developing capacity to hear the Gospel.

Penniman has, in his own work, helped us see that we can only begin where people are—with life and at the point of problem since people learn functionally and in problem situations. We do not start with Gospel, which cannot be "taught" but which happens to those who can hear the voice of the Lord speaking to them inwardly. Thus, Penniman has noted, there is a fundamental distinction between religion and education which we blur to our own confusion. Religion is the business that everyone is always engaged in of making sense out of what is by nature non-sense. Christians do this specifically in the power of Jesus as Christ. Education, on the other hand, is the process of the development of people's capacities to the point where the concrete experience of religion is enhanced so that they can make the faith response of saying "yes" to the Lord. Christian education goes on where

Christian religion is happening, but they are not the same. We are Christians by faith, not by education.

The future prospects of the Sunday school lie where they have always lain, with the decision as to the lines of curriculum development, a decision that involves prior religious decisions about the nature of the Church and the world. But how responsible can and will the Church be to its best educational understandings? Will it pay the high price for effective education and competent Sunday schools? If so, some fundamental alterations in its present understandings are required. We must be able to deliver ourselves from the outmoded theological perspectives of medieval Platonism; from a commitment to a view of man which is a denial of his freedom and his true being; from a view of education which is essentially propagandistic and indoctrinationalist, a view never held by professional educators;[12] a reductionist view of the Sunday school where teachers receive no serious training and where concern for curriculum questions and instructional methods is nearly non-existent.

There are five requirements which must be met if we are to be encouraged about the prospects for any future Christian education. First, we must grasp the meaning and carry out the implications of a radical change in direction of all our teaching. We must start where life goes on. Our people must be enabled to examine the concrete experiences of their lives. They must be helped to face the meaning of their finitude and incompleteness. Only later can we deal with the propositions and the symbols expressive of this meaning and of the mighty acts of God for men and their salvation. The radical change of direction begins with concrete human experience and moves in depth toward the discovery of the grounds of life and faith.

Second, we need to learn the disciplines of the educational

process, including the theological background and the nature of the learning process. We need to know and be able to use the technical procedure for beginning with living people and their concerns and moving through the necessary steps to the discovery of the Gospel's speaking to man in his daily life.

Third, we must eliminate the confusion between doctrine, Bible, Prayer Book, and their symbols as the objects of our teaching, and the Gospel, which can only be discovered in experience. We must master the distinction between lore and Gospel, a distinction which for education must be maintained and clarified. Only thus will we avoid making the Gospel the object of our teaching and seek to "apply" it. Lore may be taught; Gospel simply happens.

Fourth, we need freedom from the tyranny of goals. We begin with the lives of people who seek life's meaning, and where the urgency of this concern is felt and expressed. When this is done the goals will emerge relevant to the actual situation and will fasten themselves upon us. The addiction to pre-determined goals arises out of a misunderstanding of the educational process. Such goals are irrelevant and manipulative. There is no way in which we can guarantee that anyone will hear the Gospel speaking to him.

Finally, we must avoid the creationism of much present Christian education and educational materials. This becomes a presentation of a nature religion and of the logic of a supposedly ordered world in which the primary perception is that of God as creator. A sequence of historical events is substituted for the mighty acts of God in history appropriated in faith. While we know that the relationship of creation between God and the world is true, we must learn that the truth of it—its meaning—cannot be grasped outside the primary experience of redemption and of God as redeemer. If we can present only a religion of nature (pantheism) we enter into a denial of the intention to bring our people into a present relationship to the *redemptive* love of God and into the Church where the comfort of the power of His Holy Spirit will sustain us all.

If we can learn these things, the life of the Church could be renewed in our time. T. S. Eliot once wrote: ". . . the difference between the present and the past is that the conscious present is an awareness of the past in a way and to an extent which the past's awareness of itself cannot show." [13] On the other hand while the past is "altered by the present . . . the present is directed by the past." When we learn the meaning of the coinherence of present and past, of heritage and prospect, we will enable our people to be truly confirmed into the life with God in the world.

2

CHRISTIAN FORMATION OF CHILDREN AND YOUTH

BY *Dora P. Chaplin*

ONE DOUBTS if there is a reliable report on how many young people leave the Church in their teens. At one time it was said to be seven out of every ten. Some say, "They come back, bringing their children with them in later years," but look once again at the statistics, and the testimony of most of our clergy. And why are our numbers, both in parishes and theological schools, kept up by those who come in from other denominations?

Numbers are not the final yardstick. We are living in the age of the Christian *diaspora* where Christians are dispersed in a strange new world. They often gather for worship, and their whole quality of life and witness is not measurable by man.

The problem of "religious drop-outs" is a matter of the very gravest concern, but if we accept the historical fact of the scattered Church and the corporate remnant church, which in this country is sometimes obscured by dazzling figures of numerical growth, we then fit our young people more realistically into the picture. When they are confirmed, into what *quality* of Christian community are we leading them? A young person surrounded by two or three mature Christians is more likely to remain in the Church than one encompassed by hundreds of nominal Christians. He may feel lonely at school or at work as a part of the *diaspora,* but he is a part of the living, organic Church with whom he worships when it is gathered, and if he prays alone he is conscious of being a part of this community. To understand our predicament we need to look at the past, to ask what is being done in the present, and peer into the future. Some would have us begin with the Reformation, believing that nothing very significant in relation to the communication of the Gospel occurred before that; others would rush us into the twentieth century, preferably the middle of it, believing that only then did light dawn.

An early champion of parent education, the writer of Deuteronomy 6, suggests what is often announced in parish bulletins as a new idea, that religion is a part of daily life. God's people have always struggled to accept this truth.

Contemporary thinking about God and about children, called theology and psychology, are clearly reflected in the religious education of any time, especially today. We have very little account of *formal* Christian education before the Council of Trent (1545-63), but we do find letters and homilies. Most of the weight was put on parents, who were expected to be responsible. In reading the works of the saints and the fathers there is frequently a Christian voice softening the severity. An exception to this may be found in *Constitutions of the Holy Apostles* (c. 375) where the advice is given to those rearing young children: "Bring them under with cutting stripes, and make them subject from their infancy, not giving them such liberty that they get the mastery." [1] In these instructions it is interesting to notice that the *love* of God is not mentioned. Medieval schools were also the scene of cruelty from schoolmasters, and there was an attempt to inculcate religion, as well as Latin, with the rod.

During the eighteenth and nineteenth centuries, judging by what we find in museums of reading primers for little children and verses on samplers, teachers in America were influenced by the famous Jonathan Edwards, who died in 1758. He was preoccupied with original sin and referred to children as "vipers and rattlesnakes." Little can be found to remind children of their rightful place as creatures loved by God and redeemed by Christ. They were considered un-redeemed sinners until their "conversion," and were told stories of a fiery hell. Infant voices sang:

> O what pleasure 'tis to see
> Christians in harmony agree
> To teach the rising race to know
> They're born in sin, exposed to woe. [2]

By 1826 Episcopalians had their own Sunday schools, and in 1873 some attempt was made to publish lessons with teachers' helps. From that time books for the use of "the young" were largely either very dull catechisms or sickly-sweet stories of saintly children who lived, and often died, with proof-texts on their tongues, and were prayed over by numerous adults converted through their blameless lives. The materials were badly printed. Those who are discouraged about Christian education materials today should look at them; but they do convey the idea that being a Christian means that you are expected to *know* something, if only by rote, and that Christians take their beliefs seriously and act on them.

Enter: Horace Bushnell

Soon the great era of child psychology took parents by storm. As far back as 1846, Horace Bushnell, in his *Christian Nurture*, had launched his now famous idea of Christian education: "that the child is to grow up a Christian, and never know himself otherwise." He believed that the home was the most important factor in Christian formation or "nurture," that Christian beliefs could be stated through the normal happenings of daily life, that the Church and community should shoulder their responsibility in helping the growth of a child's whole personality. He fought to free children from the *artificial* and helpless sense of guilt imposed on them. Much of his teaching was later reinforced by psychological research, but Episcopalians do not seem to have taken his teaching to heart until the present century. In our quest for realism, however, we must remember how few families, even those who may be regular attendants at Church, can now be called "Christian" in the way Horace Bushnell described. Some good conservative material was produced, and courses from other denominations poured into our Sunday schools, showing the influence of John Dewey and his "child-centered curriculum." Dewey's idea that every child should be encouraged to participate *socially* was congenial to the time, and "progressive education" was a favored term.

In 1947, the National Council (now the Executive Council), was instructed by the House of Bishops to produce a "new curriculum." The Christian Education Department, with a staff of about seven officers and three secretaries, undertook the work. It was soon seen that it was more complex than anyone had imagined, and the task, now nearing the end of its second decade, has become an enterprise in budget and personnel not dreamed of by the originators. Expenses leapt from a budget, in 1947, of $131,595 to $567,081 in 1965, for a staff of twenty-seven officers and twenty-eight secretaries, with the Department of College Work, once a part of the Christian Education Department, no longer included.

The six volumes of adult books, *The Church's Teaching*, were produced by invited writers. Parish Life Weekends and Parish Life Missions were held all over the country. Visiting leaders attempted to stir both clergy and laymen to an awareness of the task of Christian education. The now popular "family service" was instituted in many parishes. Martin Buber influenced the leaders, whose speeches were full of references to his "I-Thou" teachings, and the words "sin and separation" once more became popular, as did "acceptance," and "the experience of death and resurrection." Since 1953, with a change of leadership, the influence of the social sciences, especially the "sub-science" of group dynamics, permeated the "new curriculum" at all levels. Again we see the Church's absorbing contemporary thinking and educational method. Laboratories for both clergy and laymen—even bishops!—(patterned after those held at Bethel, Maine, where the leaders were trained) were held all over North America and even in such widespread countries as England, Japan, and Australia. Typical parish situations were analyzed, and the vocabulary, which included the frequent use of such terms as "task-oriented," "group-oriented," "tactical encounter," "feed-back," "ambivalence," and "playing-it-by-ear" were used extensively in the training sessions, which examined the nature and function of small groups. These methods are implicit in the courses produced for children and young people, and in the corresponding manuals for adults. David R. Hunter says,

The organizing principle of most curriculum materials is subject matter . . . such as Church History or the Bible. The official curriculum materials of the Episcopal Church differ from other materials by employing an organizing principle providing the structure for the year's work but without timetable, schedule, or any predetermined sequence of activity. The organizing principle uses the religious issues that arise out of the action of God in people's lives—the demands He makes upon men and the offering of His reconciling love, followed by man's response, either positive or negative. . . . Each graded course in the curriculum seeks to provide the teaching team with resources which have meaning in relation to religious issues most common to the age-group with which the team is working.[3]

Unfortunately the ability to identify "religious issues" does not come overnight. It does not descend automatically upon Mrs. Jones or Mr. Smith, the parishioners who are asked to teach classes. And when a religious issue is identified, how many know what to do with it? These people need careful training (in the language of group dynamics, "in-service training") by a competent person who has himself received the proper initiation into the methods used. Only a very small percentage of the clergy, even if they are among those who have had a glimpse of the principles and their use in the various conferences held for them, have the time to teach the teachers. Few parishes have directors of Christian education, and not all of these leaders give sufficient time to the individual teacher. Diocesan training conferences are poorly attended. Many parishes use one or more courses from the *Seabury Series* and leave the teachers to sink or swim on their own, taking the pupils along with them. The revised courses, however, do offer more specific help to the teachers, and are divided into units. The teaching "team" is still expected to be two people, the teacher and an "associate" (no longer called an "observer," but he still "observes"). But the fact remains that few teachers are receiving any help other than from books. Moreover, most teachers have only twenty to thirty-five minutes for the lesson, making significant achievement well-nigh impossible. A Church lulled to sleep by imposing and expensive new educational buildings, big enrollments in Sunday Church schools, and beautifully printed books would receive a shock if it stopped to think about the new situation.

Although the *Seabury Series* is the "official curriculum" of the Episcopal Church, it has by no means been universally accepted. The majority of our parishes continue to use a variety of independently produced lesson materials, ranging from the conservative to the *avant garde,* and uneven in quality.

Reason for Teaching

Fortunately God does not depend entirely upon the printed word for the communication of the Gospel. Inherent in much of our methodology is the danger that we shall lose sight of our *reason* for teaching, which should be to discover God in Christ and to transform our lives to His purpose. Methods are only vehicles for conveying truth; they must not be confused with the truth itself. The communication of the Christian faith is often confused with the teaching of other "subjects." I have dealt with this frequently in my own writings, and the Abbé Marc Oraison supports the same view when he says,

> A religious education that is really consistent with the receptive potentialities of the child and with the work of God . . . consists in encouraging the child to enter into a personal and living relationship with Someone. This Someone, in this dia-

logue which He seeks in the very heart of man, has His Word to say.[4]

Preoccupation with method leads to concern for a *scheme* rather than with a Person. This tendency, which points to an attenuated form of Christianity, often without God except by vague inference, and certainly without hope, is increasing today. We hear the word "relevance" *ad nauseum,* and when a brave voice says, "Relevant to what?" there should be a stronger one crying, "Relevant to Whom?"

Exactly what opportunities will our children have to be "formed" into mature, witnessing Christians? Ideally, they will have parents who anticipate their birth with joy, surround them with an unselfish love which enables them to know and recognize the love of God when they are in the nursery, and to deepen that knowledge by faith and teaching as the years go on. There are parents who, although they know themselves to be sinners, are also aware of being *forgiven sinners,* who not only attend church but love God and are able to worship him, with the congregation and in private, and who study the Bible. Such parents love their neighbors without prejudice and are zealous in their work for the Kingdom. With parents like these, to whom God is obviously important, the child has continuing support for any formal teaching that the Church may offer. Or he may have parents who themselves are only now beginning to learn what Christianity is. There is no need for them to be far along the road; what matters to the child is that they care, and that they can travel along the road with him. Let us assume that we have assent to the statement that the teaching of the Christian faith, especially on the deepest levels of consciousness, is best done at home, particularly in the early years, combined with the experience of Sunday worship in "the family of God."

But the Church must also minister to the unwanted child; to the overindulged child who is still unloved; to the child crowded into a few feet of space in a tenement, who does not know who his father is; to the one, rich or poor, who has never had a loving relationship with an adult; to the child whose set of values is based purely on material possessions; to the one rejected because of race, a broken body, emotional damage, or a retarded mind. These are our children. They come from religious homes in name or reality; from broken homes, pagan homes, or "do-not-know" homes where the parents think it would be good for them to have some religion. Acknowledging all these conditions and differences, what chance does the modern child have (who does not attend a parish day school) to hear the Gospel and respond to it?

1. Through his Baptism if it is taken seriously. Later, through the grace of the Holy Communion. (Are his parents helpful, obstructive, or indifferent?)

2. Through his growing experience of God in worship and prayer. (Who will guide him here?)

3. Through the "contagion of faith" communicated by a teacher who will lead a class twenty to forty minutes once a week for up to forty Sundays a year, if the parents send him regularly and do not go away for too many weekends. (Does he have such a teacher? Are the adults receiving any help?) Through any happy contact in the parish family, with priest or layman.

4. Through careful preparation for Confirmation, devoted post-Confirmation teaching, youth fellowships which are truly fellowships, wise spiritual direction, good youth conferences, and ably-led retreats. (Are there opportunities available?) Through vacation Church school. Through "released time" classes (where they are effectively taught).

6. Through Christian art, drama, and literature. (Who is supplying him with this?) In a recent English report on "The Purposes of Broadcasting" the statement is made that "triviality is more dangerous to the soul than wickedness."

7. Through opportunities not only to see witnessing, useful lives, but to serve others and to become ready for the joy and hurt of witnessing. (What is the depth of worship, knowledge, and witness in the adults around him? What opportunities for growth and guidance do *they* have?)

8. Through being helped to see God in Christ at work in history, and in the *good* forces at work in today's world. (Who is helping him here?)

A new mentality has been created in youth, and a constant euphoria is sought after. "Happiness, success, freedom," are the keywords, and all must pursue these goals. In spite of all this, the teen-age world is empty. They tell me that they "want to get out of it," they dance "rock-'n'-roll," or whatever "the latest" is, finding some release in the booming and the crashing uproar; others resort to whatever escape they find at hand to express their mistaken freedom—dangerous speed, too much drink, irresponsible and often loveless sex, and drugs.

All this is symptomatic. If the Church is going to minister to its children and youth—and the Church is you and I, adult members of it—we need the *grace* to see that many young people today are not merely confused but deeply wounded. We cannot love unless we understand; and unless there is mutual respect between teacher and taught, we shall simply increase the gap. Disillusioned and shocked young people need adults to guide them who can help and reassure. This cannot be done through our own "natural" power. It will come only as we and other adults open up our lives to the grace and truth of our Lord, Jesus Christ.

The Life of Worship

The Episcopal Church has particular treasures and resources in its liturgical life. This is an hour of great opportunity, and instead of clinging to the despondency of the disciples at the hour of the Crucifixion, we must learn to live in the light of the Resurrection. The young need to see us in a recognizable, total witness. Christianity is not just an idea, it is an *event*. Many young people who have been *helped by all the resources at our disposal* are able to commit their lives to Christ at their Confirmation, and have a tremendous aptitude for an increasing recognition of God as life goes on. It is true that they are not yet able to recognize sin as the abysmal evil that it is, although they encounter it and have their times of despondency. Still they can be led to the sources of forgiveness and restoration *if only the adults around them know that these gifts exist!* The frightening aspect is not so much the behavior of youth as the superficiality and ignorance of those adults who are denouncing or ignoring, when they should be ministering. Young people do not want to be marshalled into big organizations so much as to have a chance to be themselves in small groups under wise guidance, meeting not just to discuss problems, but to be together in work and play if they wish. They need to see relaxed and joyful commitment in their elders.

Today when such a high value is set on the group that it amounts to idolatry, we must not lose sight of the need for much individual pastoral work which can and must be done by mature Christian laymen as well as clergy. The great, decisive battles of God are frequently fought out in this way.

It is possible to be quite learned in the theoretical side of teaching yet to miss the central reality of faith. For example, much course material referring to Baptism reveals a shallow and one-sided theology which leaves out God's action in the sacrament. Baptism is concerned with "that which *by nature* we cannot have." It is related to the supernatural, or what is better described as spiritual reality.

A few years ago I wrote,

> The underlying principle in the life of worship cannot be brushed aside without tragic consequences. If we take time to question confirmands we often find that they have come to divide the universe into two spheres, the spiritual and the material, and of the two, the material to them is *real*. They have no awareness of the world where the spiritual and the material are mysteriously clothed with the outward and the visible; yet this is the world in which we live. . . . God chooses outward forms to convey inner meanings, even the gift of Himself.[5]

This is all true from babyhood onward. If our much-scolded parents can be helped to see that the atmosphere of personal, loving relationship and in the ordinary, common events of daily life, among all the scattered people of God, Monday through Saturday, are all an important part of the life of the Church and the "formation" of children and youth as well as ourselves, they will not think of Christianity as something belonging only to Sunday and to be expressed only in religious language. They will gather on Sunday, offer themselves and receive grace at the altar, and be reminded of their baptismal life. The world will *not* be neatly divided into the sacred and secular.

How? How can we respond to the gifts of love and grace God holds out to us? If we want to mature spiritually, we must experience the necessary processes of nurture.

Adults must grow up in their inner lives. Thoughtful books

are needed, suggesting concrete and realistic methods of responding to the gifts of grace and love described by the "new theologians" as being held out by God to man. We must examine what Bonhoeffer meant by "the secret discipline," and ask how modern young people can face the apparently impossible task of living out in a secular world what seem to them vague theories. How dare we present them with what we believe to be a Christian ethic when we give them no method of response or certainty of direction? We offer them sociology and humanism alone, disguised under the cloak of a few religious terms. We expect them to leap from the acceptance of some religious proclamation to the battle of carrying it out without the necessary bridge of the grace mediated to us by a living God, a "contemporary Christ," through the means which He, not we, has chosen. These means include prayer.

Martin Thornton blazed the trail in 1965 with *The Rock and the River*, in which he shows the bridge which can be built between traditional spirituality and the "new theology." He says:

> Christian life in response to the love of God is a "process," formal prayers are "events" or "encounters" with God, and once the doctrine of the organic Church is accepted, then the liturgy and the office constitute an existential "concrete situation" in which the whole of one's being is involved. But when this is rejected, we return to the Protestant jump from existential situations straight into ethics; the central concepts of "choice" and "commitment" can only be interpreted in terms of practical behavior. If the doctrines of grace, of the Holy Spirit, of encounter with the living Word are not to be jettisoned—and these are Protestant hall-marks—then *ethics must be mediated through, and reunited with, prayer in the ethic-ascetic synthesis of prayer.* It is curious that the

splitting up of this synthesis is the prevailing pastoral error of both modern Protestantism and of the Council of Trent! [6]

Is it any wonder that our young people are confused, and leave the Church, when they are tossed into a sea of conflicting beliefs? Modern life inflicts changes of abode on our youngsters. In one parish they may be asked to keep to some unrealistic rule of life, fostering a false sense of guilt, and in the next told that "this old-fashioned pietism is nonsense." We are not going to give our children the fullest basis for "entering into" Christ (not merely having a polite or impolite acquaintanceship) until they are nurtured in the three-fold life of prayer on which worship in the liturgical Christian churches is based; that is, the Eucharist, the office, and personal prayer.

Bishop John A. T. Robinson says, "To pray for another is to expose both oneself and him to the common ground of our being; it is to see one's concern for him in terms of *ultimate* concern." [7] This describes an advanced type of intercession, for which solid foundations must be built. It is cruel to hold up such an ideal before a person of any age when he has had no practical help in attaining it. In the Episcopal Church there is a tragic dearth of realistic books on the inner life of worship and prayer for *modern young people,* also of non-sentimental ones for children. A stream of men leaving our seminaries know a lot *about* God and the Bible, but are unequipped as teachers of prayer or as spiritual directors because their own experience of the life of prayer is nil.

We know too well about the dangers and destruction in the modern world. Yet these are exciting times in which to be growing up in the Church. They are days of ecumenical hope, of liturgical enthusiasm, of the awareness of social issues, of a whole new dimension of life and recognition for the laity. We cannot allow our young people to grow up as "apostles of despair" because adults have become indifferent, despondent, or arrogant. Our young people are waiting to take part in the renewal of the Church. To guide them, we need more rebels, more gifted rebels, more God-gifted rebels. We need more saints whose lives are bound up with the *present* life of the Son of God.

3

THE PARISH EDUCATIONAL STRUCTURE

BY *Kendig Brubaker Cully*

WHEN we use the word "parish" today, it is not often that the origin of the word comes to mind. It is derived ultimately from the Greek *paroikia*, which connotes "dwelling beside" or "sojourning." The parish is the company of Christians dwelling within the secular city, or, in the words of Daniel B. Stevick, "a 'foreign quarter,' a stranger in the city of man—set there for the redemption and the judgment of the community." [1] Looked at from another standpoint, one can construe the parish as having no meaning apart from its relationship to the diocese, just as a diocese, a geographical manifestation of the Church, has no significance in itself apart from its relationship to the total Body of Christ, the universal Church.

To most Americans "parish" means the particular congregation to which one belongs. In an earlier day a great deal of attention was paid to the geographical boundaries of parishes. It was assumed that all baptized persons within the bounds of a parish would be associated with its life and worship. Nowadays, especially in view of contemporary mobility within areas, considerable re-thinking has been going on to determine just how the concept of a parish can be entertained in our present culture.[2]

The Educative Parish

This is not to suggest that the idea of "parish" is about to be abandoned. In a very real sense every Christian must be attached to a local company of Christians if he is to exercise his calling in the faith, for a full-fledged Christian in isolation is unthinkable. Even the chronically shut-in person whose physical impediments might prevent his worshipping in the nave on Sundays or participating in group meetings outside his own home will be deeply related, if his Christian profession is taken seriously, through prayer and contact of one sort or another to a local congregation of the faithful.

Furthermore, it is in the local parish that truly educative relationships and learnings take place. A national Church or even a diocese can provide over-all strategies and even some profitable aids for the Christian growth of persons, but these must be appropriated and shared within an intimate, tangible company if they are to assist toward growing faith and Christian action.

How effective, then, is the local parish in serving as the educative medium through which primary Christian learnings will take place?

In order to assess a local parish thus, we have to look at the structure within which parish life operates in the context of the Episcopal Church. It goes without saying, to anyone who is even vaguely familiar with the way Episcopal parishes operate, that the clergyman is a key figure in this regard. The canons are actually rather generalized with regard to a rector's educational responsibility. He is bidden to catechize the children and inform his people regarding the doctrine, worship, and mission of the Church. It is his function to instruct the sponsors in Holy Baptism and prepare confirmands for presentation to the Bishop.[3] Apart from the scant description of his duties in the official laws of the Church, however, the inevitable outgrowth of such primary assigned responsibilities has been that he has become the very nerve-center of whatever is undertaken in his parish. It is unlikely that most rectors would be happy to delegate to someone else, or even to a committee, *total* responsibility for the selection of a Church school curriculum, for example, any more than they would completely resign the supervision of music in the services to even a most competent professional musician.

This primary prerogative which lies with the rector is not an unmixed blessing, however, with regard to educational efficiency and outcomes in a parish. If a particular rector is not interested in Christian education, or assigns it to a low place on his roster of duties, the likelihood is that the whole parish's educational feeling-tone and practice will suffer. On the other hand, he may be so jealous of his *rights* in the matter that he will fail to recognize the willingness and capacities of others, even theologically trained curates, to do effective work in the very areas where he is uninterested or weak.

Fortunately, due to deeper understandings of groups and how they function which have been penetrating the Church, there is evidence that a more serious educational purpose has come to the attention of many pastors within the last two decades. The authoritarian personality often has been found to be a failure, whereas the clergyman who trusts his lay people and shares the ministry in Christ with them in areas of *their* competence turns out usually to be the one whose parish will develop a genuinely educational quality, encouraging people to grow in faith and practice even as they exercise *their* part in the *magisterium* of Christ's priesthood.

One way in which a rector can function with educational effectiveness is to create a Christian education committee or board within his parish. This will fail if it is considered to be only "advisory" or "consultative." One has known of a parish in a sophisticated suburban city where such a committee was recruited from extremely capable lay people who had wide influence not only in their local community but nationally, and included among their number some theologically very literate people as well as others conversant with a wide range of educational problems. That committee was short-lived because they soon discovered that the rector merely wanted them as a rubber-stamp, to give seeming prestige to *his* preconceptions. A committee must be given genuine authority, in trust, by the rector. There is little reason to believe that the rector's canonical controls would suffer by his willingness to provide an authentic task for such a committee to do, along with the power to implement their decisions. If he is theologically competent himself, he need not fear that such a group will usurp his prerogatives; rather, they will be receptive to all possible teaching that he himself, by virtue of his theological training and perceptivity, can give them.

Staff Responsibilities

Another area of difficulty that sometimes arises in Episcopal parishes is the unwillingness or incapacity of the rector to share responsibilities with his staff. Every large-sized parish nowadays faces the need for specialized leadership from a director of Christian education. Sometimes such a director will be a curate, a recent seminary graduate who has been granted Holy Orders. Oftentimes these young curates are sufficiently enthusiastic and versatile to do an amazingly good job in the Church school or youth groups. Fortunately the seminaries have been improving their teaching in the discipline of Christian education in recent years, and few young bachelors of divinity emerge from the seminary without at least a foundational course in this field. On the other hand, youthful exuberance and a willingness to learn are scarcely adequate to cope with the demanding requirements of a large parish Sunday school, involving as it does constant teacher-counseling, familiarity with curricular materials, skill in group work, as well as managerial efficiency. The rector needs seriously to examine his own conscience to see if he really intends to develop a creative parish program of Christian education, or if he is chiefly interested in having an ordained man on the staff who will help with services, calling, and the multitude of details, sandwiching the Church school between sets of other responsibilities. The time factor in the appointment of curates is another relevant consideration. If it is intended that a curacy shall last no more than two or three years, and is regarded as primarily a learning experience for the young minister, is there much likelihood that any really serious educational effort will be expended or any profound confrontation with the parish dimension effected?

The alternative in a large parish is to engage a woman as director of Christian education. It is noteworthy that some of the most creative educational leaders in parish life have been women. However, here, too, problems exist. Obviously, only a professionally trained woman can do an adequate job as director. Is the rector willing and able to admit that women, too, can be theologically competent? (Seminary professors often have observed that women students frequently outclass their male counterparts, due perhaps to the fact that only a relatively few women choose to study theology,

and consequently are likely to be at the top of their undergraduate college classes, whereas the top men of college
graduating classes find their way to seminaries in smaller
numbers.) Many rectors seem to have a deep-seated distrust
of women theologians, even though such women graduates
often have demonstrated a natural aptitude for working
with children, youth, and adults, in a creative and productive
way. (Few men, except for those of the stature of a Pestalozzi or a Froebel, have excelled in working with very young
children, for example.)

All this is of course part of a larger problem within the
Episcopal Church—an *educational,* but also a moral, problem—viz., when and how can women be granted their
proper New Testament status as co-equals with men in the
life of the Church? In defense of the clergy on this score, it
must be remembered that the Bishops and clergy in recent
General Conventions have been on the side of the women
with regard to full participation in the Convention as deputies, whereas the opposition has lain with the lay deputies.

In many respects the Episcopal Church has lagged far
behind other American Church bodies in the status accorded
to professionally educated directors of Christian education.[4]

Too many parishes have been willing to confer that title
on women who have some managerial competence but who
lack the subtle understandings and technical background
that only a program of graduate study in a seminary or university divinity school can provide. The result has been an
ambivalence on the part of many young women as to
whether they care to invest their God-given talents in a
Church vocation in view of the uncertain roles they may
be expected by both clergy and vestrymen to perform. This
whole question needs more frank facing than the Church
has yet shown any willingness to undertake.

The Imperative to Teach

Granted that many problems of the type we have discussed above exist, still it is in the parish that the climate for education can be established, the pursuit of educational excellence fostered, and the immediate responsibility falling on the local group of Christians to go into the world and teach the nations discharged. Falling back on professionally safeguarded vested interests or outmoded concepts of what Christian involvement means is untenable for any parish to be content with any longer. The teaching imperative for the Church as it faces a world whose daily life tends to bypass previously held convictions must be infinitely more pervasive of the whole of parish life than ever before in history. The alternative is horrendous for sensitive believers to contemplate.[5]

4

CHOICE AND UTILIZATION OF CURRICULUM

BY *Max M. Pearse, Jr.*

BEFORE we can choose a curriculum with any success, we shall have to know what one is. The word "curriculum" is of Latin ancestry and it originally meant "race course." Some early teacher must have thought the race track a good analogy for organized study. Race tracks are enclosed. Like them, organized study should fence off some particular area for study. Race tracks are also planned to take the runner through different parts of the enclosed field, just as organized study should. Broadly understood, then, curriculum means an organized plan of study to take learners through different parts of a given "field."

Later teachers used the term in two different ways. Some had in mind a single "course" (Church history, for instance) when they talked about curriculum. Other teachers used curriculum to mean the whole bundle of courses which might go to make up a single educational program. When we speak of curriculum in this chapter, we are using the word to stand for a total program, made up of different "courses."

Preconditions for Curriculum

After definition, comes the job of understanding some preconditions for curriculum. In other words, we must understand that certain things need to happen before any curriculum can begin to succeed, and we must try to make their acquaintance. (It is of no use to buy a particular series of courses, for instance, if our Church school has no students.) Many a parish has rejected a given series on the unexamined assumption that every curriculum should be a substitute for its own preconditions. (In other words, a series of courses is blamed for the fact that our Church school has no students.)

Lists of preconditions are bound to vary. Even so, three preconditions for curriculum choice seem too essential to escape comment.

The first is a strong devotional life in the parish. Consideration of prayer may seem out of place in a chapter focused on curriculum. But is not prayer the food of the Church's ministry, and is not Christian education a prime component of this ministry? If the answer to these two questions is "yes," a third question seems in order: How can a Church school perform any of its functions (including curriculum choice) without prayer?

Before we turn to curriculum then, we might well ask: Is the ministry of our Church school the subject of individual and corporate prayer by the people of this congregation? Prayer failure may be a telling symptom of real carelessness about the educational ministry of Christ's Church. A good deal of banal, unworthy curricular material finds its way into parishes because those responsible are willing to settle for the easiest choice. Such a group's real criteria are to be found among questions like these: Is the material stocked locally? Is it material we are used to? Does it make life easy for us by eliminating as much thought and effort as possible? None of these shoddy questions can survive a climate of prayer.

A second precondition for good curriculum choice may also strike the reader as far afield from the subject; it is what we might call a "sense of commission." We need to have made clear to us the fact that we are "under orders" to teach—that to accept Christianity is to accept the discipline of a teaching commission. It seems possible to infer three simple, important ideas about teaching Christianity if we look into the New Testament:

1. We are told to teach. In Matthew 28:19, 20 we read, "Go, therefore, and make disciples of all nations, baptizing them in the name of the Father, and of the Son, and of the Holy Spirit, *teaching* them to observe all that I have commanded you. . . ."

2. We, as a Christian people, will be able to teach. The parishioner with least schooling in our own parish has probably had more educational advantages than most of our Lord's original apostles.

3. Our failure to teach is taken seriously. We read, for example, in Mark 9:42, "Whoever causes one of these little ones who believe in me to sin, it would be better for him if a great millstone were hung around his neck, and he were thrown into the sea." It seems at least possible to reason that one way to "cause sin" in "little ones" is to deny them teaching.

Such statements as these are not meant to make up a completely adequate theology of education, but rather to stand as a second buttress against shallow or lazy investments in the choosing of curriculum. We are about the Lord's business as surely in the committee room as at the Eucharist.

Seen in perspective, a lively devotional life and a sense of the teaching commission may turn out to be the most important elements in good curriculum decision.

Spiritual commitment ought to inspire, not replace, practical understanding. So it is not out of place to put down parochial survey as a third precondition to the choosing process. This fact-gathering about parish education can be widespread and elaborate, or simple and limited, but we have to have it. Until we know what kind of material we have, we cannot know what tools are best for its shaping.

We might begin our inquiry into the educational program of our parish by looking into the concrete, tangible side of our school. Here are some sample questions: How much can we budget for printed curriculum? How much for activity materials and reference books? How much schooling do most of our teachers have? Must each teacher go it alone or will she have a team mate? Will class space and furniture support activities (other than lecture and discussion)?

While the kinds of questions we have just asked have their place, we should not stop with them. The facts most important for the reception of curriculum probably lie in the intangible realm of attitude and relationship. An "intangibles survey" might include such queries as these: How important is the Church school in the rector's program? Where do the director of Christian education, the Church school superintendent, the teachers, and the students fit into the status structure of the parish? (This question should, of course, be pursued in terms of action, not theory.) Does the superintendent, for instance, have first choice of the persons with the best talent in the parish for teacher recruitment, or have they already been persuaded to commit themselves as ushers? What image of the Church school do parents mediate to their children? (How much priority does Church school attendance have over weekends at the cottage in good weather?) The point is not that these very questions be used, but that this kind of questioning be respected.

Before we even begin the choosing process, then, we would do well to consider the condition of our devotional life, our commitment to a teaching commission, and our understanding of a given parish.

Choosing a Curriculum

We come now to the process of choosing a curriculum. The ingredients of this process are time, criteria, and the material itself.

There is no quick way to choose a good curriculum. Committees would do well to ponder this simple but important fact at the outset of their work. Any time saved in rushing ill-adapted material to the parish will soon be lost in the endless new vexations of recruitment, morale, administration, and promotion which it invites. And this is the situation in too many of our parishes. No one, in fact, may know very much about the curriculum in use. It arrived in the parish hard on the heels of a last-minute decision to "get something ready for the fall" or to pacify the most easily recruited teachers. If we do not have time to plan for our Church schools, we would do far better to close them.

My own guess is that a year would seem none too long to spend in curricular study before choosing. (We will always be at the disposal of the most superficial complaints unless we are knowledgeable enough about our choice to defend it.)

There are probably as many criteria for the choosing of curricula as there are people writing on the subject. My own conviction is this: If the needs of four different kinds of people can be met by a given course or series, it deserves a chance in our parish. The four kinds of people whose needs might well shape our choice are: the theologian, the administrator, the teacher, and the learner. (The reason for considering these people in this particular order will be taken up later.)

The needs of the theologian are to be met for the simple reason that curriculum exists to satisfy the teaching commission of the Church and to mediate its heritage. If a curriculum does not do this job, what other reason could justify its existence?

By "theologian," we do not mean that every parish should import a seminary professor for consultation. It is usually reasonable that the rector consider this his job. He has been entrusted with graduate education in theology and committed to responsibility for the educational work of his parish by the canon law of the church.

Once enlisted, the theologian will probably make his start with the official statements of purpose which usually preface a series or course. If, for instance, he finds in the purpose an idea of Scripture as the literal, word-by-word dictation of the Almighty, he will probably want to abandon the course or series.

Besides an over-all series goal, each course ought to state clearly what it is trying to do. These goals need also to be checked, both in terms of the theology which they set forth themselves, and the way in which they fit together to serve the greater goal.

Looking into the stated purposes of a course, however, is only half the theologian's job. The other half concerns the kind of theology which emerges through the literature and methodology of the course. (In other words, are what a course says it teaches and what it actually does teach the same?) Questions like these are certainly in order: Are people presented in the stories believable in terms of the Christian doctrine of man as both sinner and child of God? Are the children in the stories "too good to be true"? Are the ethical choices oversimplified to the point of irrelevance in our own difficult world? (Would children get the idea that in this fallen creation we really have a choice between "black" and "white" rather than between two shades of "gray"?) Would children get ideas of God they would later have to unlearn?

Just as a course's real theology comes out in its stories, it can be hunted down quite easily through the methods advocated and the advice given to the teacher. How much Christian concern for our fellow man, for instance, is reflected in a kindergarten course which assumes that kindergartners will sit at small tables through the entire period, as though they were college students? Similarly, from time to time, one may find suggestions in the material that the teacher is to "put one over" on the students. He is to "bring the discussion around to . . ." this or that point of view. Most of us would agree that a teacher has a right and duty to state facts (e.g., the wording of the Apostles' Creed) without holding a class plebiscite for their ratification. Further, the teacher has a right and duty to speak his own mind. But to pretend to give a class freedom and then to manipulate them toward the teacher's point of view—this betrays a shoddy depreciation of the human being whom God has created.

Of course, there is no end to the clues which a lesson series can supply to a theologian.

After the theologian, we might well consider the administrator's part in the choosing process. By administrator, we simply mean the man (or woman) who keeps the Church school under way by providing for its operating needs. He will usually be called a superintendent and ideally will have had some administrative seasoning from his own career. True, a great deal of his time will be taken up with tangible questions. But we will ignore his importance to the Church school only if we discount the sacramental principle of our faith. (We say we believe that material things—bread and wine—can be the vehicles for important spiritual realities.) A dirty, cluttered classroom may well talk to a child like this: "We adults only pretend to take Christianity seriously. Actually, we don't count it for much. Just look at the kind of room we have provided for its study."

Practically, of course, the administrator's questions are crucial for the actual survival of a given curriculum in a given parish, and they should be asked early in the choosing process. Here is a sampling of the questions he might raise: How much does the lesson series cost? Do we need a reader for every pupil? Are paper and binding strong enough to outlast a single year? How dependent is the course on expensive activity and reference resources outside itself? Even if we can afford them, are the kits and reference books readily available? Could we store the material easily or is there a welter of supplemental resources, all of differing sizes and shapes, to be forced into the stubborn uniformity of our shelf size? Will the material "keep" any length of time? (Do frequent revisions obliterate our investment in the materials themselves or in the training of teachers for a particular course?) Questions too mundane to deserve our notice? No. It is simple common sense to ask whether we can afford a curriculum, or staff it, or house it before we rush too glibly for an order blank.

After the theologian and administrator comes the teacher in our consideration (but not in rank of importance). No one else is as important to the learner. Much depends on his being satisfied with the material chosen: how effectively he teaches, his own morale while teaching, his future availability for the teaching job. So his questions, and the categories they represent, had better be taken seriously.

First might come questions about the philosophy (or reasoning) behind a course. A typical teacher might ask: Do I understand why this particular content is to be taught and these methods advocated? (If the course represents a point of view new to me, am I helped to understand and appreciate it?) Am I helped to see how this particular course works together with its neighbors to serve a consistent, over-all master goal?

Next, the teacher might ask some questions about content: Is it really suited to the age level of the youngsters I will be teaching? (Developmental characteristics ought to be spelled out simply and vividly in the teacher's manual.) Is it clear how all of the content material of the course serves its content goal? Do I respect the stories and explanations given?

Still later, one might turn to the methods implicit in a course or series. Do the methods advocated square with the official goal? The same question we considered earlier is again in point. (For instance, does the official goal proclaim God's care for all His children, only to have the same course advocate manipulation of these same children so that the discussion will "come out right"?) Are the methods advocated realistic for a teacher of my background and experience? Are new methods justified and explained clearly enough to encourage my experimentation with them? Are there enough definite suggestions in the book to carry me through "dry times" (in myself and in the class) when we do not feel inventive or spontaneous?

After a teacher has taken a beginning glance at the "philosophy," "content," and "method" of a course, his curiosity ought not to be exhausted. The following questions may indicate its range: Is there understandable discussion about discipline? If I am to have a team mate in my teaching, is each of our roles presented clearly? (If the second member of the team is to act as an observer, is this role justified and explained to a newcomer?) Can I get at the books, audiovisual aids, and other activity materials suggested through adequate supply listings? Can I see myself and the children getting real satisfaction out of the course work as presented?

Finally, we come to the learner, himself; it is here that we encounter a strange paradox. Everyone would agree, in principle, that it is for the learner's success that the curriculum committee exists. Yet, how many times, in the reader's experience, have learners themselves actually been invited to help choose curriculum? The learner is bound to have data that will elude the theologian, the administrator, and the teacher. He deserves a solid part in the decision for which he will bear the major brunt.

It is hazardous to speak for learners. They are the largest group we have to consider, and they inevitably include the broadest range of interests and traits. Still, an imaginary learner might represent a fair number of his fellows when asking some such questions as these: Do I understand the thinking behind the course? (In other words, what are we supposed to be learning and how are we supposed to be doing it?) Is there real leeway for my individuality, or am I continually subsumed under generalizations about "the sixth-grade child"? Do the methods of the course use different kinds of learning abilities or are all the methods dedicated to the verbal learner? Does the course depend on a lot of help at home, penalizing children who lack family support? How well would the course stand up in terms of organization, art work, binding, printing, etc. when compared with a public school course for the same grade? (Granted, children might not put their questions into the same words we have used; these issues may still be important for them.)

We have discussed the needs of the theologian, administrator, teacher, and learner in precisely this order because it has a kind of logic. If, for example, the curriculum does not teach the heritage of the Church (theologian) why bother with it at all? If, in turn, we cannot afford it, why consult teachers? Finally, if teachers cannot understand it, it is not likely to be shared with learners. This order is, however, not implacable. One can easily imagine teachers and students so impressed with a given curriculum (which the administrator has vetoed because of cost) that they get the budget re-examined.

If then, a definition of "curriculum" is understood, if Christian foundations for curricular choice are respected, if the condition of the parish is known, and if the proper questions of theologian, administrator, teacher, and pupil are consulted, we have supplied important ingredients for effective choice.

Utilizing a Curriculum

Everything which would make for successful teaching belongs to our work as curriculum users. The range of topics is far beyond the scope of this chapter. The following list is a skeletal indication of what we must do to give any curriculum a fair trial in our parish:

1. We must involve the congregation in the religious life of the parish.
2. We should build a background of information through survey.
3. We should make some plan for the educational work of our parish or mission.
4. We need to make a thoughtful decision about curriculum.
5. We need to recruit the best teachers possible.
6. Teachers should be introduced to their work and maintained in it through adequate training.
7. We should support our teachers through administration.

8. Our results with curriculum need to be regularly and carefully evaluated.
9. The missionary commission of the church school to attract and hold new learners needs to be pursued.

An additional problem needs to be mentioned before we set out to discuss utilization in a more specific way. Religious curriculum points properly to everything in a learner's life which would teach him about religion (the worship of his parish, the attitude of his parents, etc.). In this section we will use the word "curriculum" to mean a series of Church school courses reflecting some central plan (*The Episcopal Church Fellowship Series* or *The Seabury Series,* for instance.)

With this preface in mind, we will choose from the larger list three educational responsibilities for consideration: teacher training, administration, and evaluation.

Teacher training, strictly speaking, would probably include only those dealings with a teacher meant to get him ready for his classroom work. But teachers need to be nurtured in their classroom work, as well as prepared for it, if they are to be really trained. In addition, no teacher is apt to teach to his full potential unless supported by pastoral encouragement and parochial response. So training can really point to three functions: "training proper," pastoral maintenance, and parochial response.

Training proper does not depend on any one setting for its success. The traditional recipe of a few sessions in the fall to train the teachers in one parish can be varied endlessly:

1. Parishes can unite in such a way that all fifth-grade teachers from the associated parishes form a single training class, as do all the sixth-grade teachers, etc.
2. The ecumenical training program of the Council of

Churches can be used with supplementary meetings for the teachers in a given Episcopal parish.

3. Closed circuit television, films, or filmstrips can provide a general introduction to the curriculum (or the specific grade) with a local trainer adding the specific help needed for a given parish.

But the design which appeals most strongly to the writer is training through consultation: teachers are trained in week by week conferences (bi-weekly at the least) with a a trainer. The approach has several advantages. The trainer can draw on the emerging classroom experience of his teachers for the training program itself. He can deal with his teachers' puzzlements as they are born, week by week (rather than with their awesome accumulation over a whole semester). He can befriend and encourage the teacher at the onset of his discouragement (rather than wait until it has developed into a full-blown determination to resign). Most important, the trainer can give his teachers the kind of education they can absorb. When we go into new territory we appreciate step-by-step help. Guidance with next Sunday's lesson is about as big a helping of educational wisdom as most of us can manage. For the same reason, we need specific aid for our own fifth-grade class, not the problems of the Church school in general.

Nothing so useful as consultation should be dismissed as "impractical for our parish." In a small Church school the rector might be able to meet for half an hour with all his teaching teams at least every other week. In a large parish he, or his trainer, could work intensively with a few especially promising teachers with the understanding that they, in turn, would train others. A good many parishes have unsuspected trainer-talent on their rolls—a retired teacher or counselor, a mother largely housebound with young children who might do some teacher training in her living room.

Nor should the consultation idea be given up because it requires some complicated agenda. True, trainers will be immeasurably helped if they can have special orientation. But consultation can begin with such a simple schedule as this: What was the lesson plan for last Sunday (either the teacher's or the manual's or a combination of the two)? What actually happened to the plan in class? What suggestions does this experience give us for next week's planning?

Just as important in terms of teacher morale (psychologists might well say "more important") as "training proper" is pastoral support. We have already noticed how this can be built into a consultation program. However teachers are listened to, befriended, or encouraged, they will probably need this kind of support to survive. Recurrent prayer for the sacrificial ministries of teachers and frequent pastoral calls on them ought to have a high priority with the parish priest. In our culture particularly, teaching and learning are far too lonely.

Finally, every teacher deserves the kind of parochial response that can maintain his morale. True, the great satisfaction roots in his devotional life (in the satisfaction of having tried to respond to God's love). But we are all creatures of a temporal world as well as a spiritual one. So some concrete expressions of appreciation by the parish are certainly in order. For instance, in one Church school the vestry gave the teachers a fine dinner party at the close of the year. "Class parents" might be encouraged to help their children thank the teacher. The form of our appreciation is not so important. The spirit it manifests is vital.

After training, the writer would put administration as the chief helper of good curriculum use. In the minds of many, it calls up visions of grubby and marginal detail work, but without good administration no curriculum has a chance.

The responsibilities, or "job description" of the average

Church school teacher is a good example. One suspects that a good many Church schools have condemned a given curriculum without bothering to find out whether the teacher ever had a chance to teach it. Most Church schools could be immeasurably helped were they to bring some administrative talent to the question, "What do we have a right to expect from a volunteer Church school teacher?" Certainly, lesson preparation, actual teaching, and involvement in a training program when necessary—these might comprise our first list. We might next logically ask ourselves, "If the teacher did these jobs well, how many other things could he take on?" Finally, we might put the sobering question, "How much is the teacher actually expected to do in our parish?" Is he expected to prepare his own room? Take all the transportation and supervisory responsibilities for his field trips? Deal unaided with guerilla warriors in the class? Raise extra money with a booth at the Church school fair? Interrupt his course with a special study program during Lent? Without an administrator to befriend him, a teacher may be surrounded and defeated by the sheer number of thoughtless demands.

In addition to the quantity of demands made on a teacher, the administrator will be concerned about other working conditions: Is there really enough space for much besides passive sitting in our classrooms? (We do not always need a new building program to get more space. A staggered class schedule, rumpus rooms in neighboring houses—even moving the cloak rack into the hall, may do wonders for our space problem.) Is there enough time for our classes? Further, is this time reasonably protected from interruptions? (The superintendent does not have to disrupt classes in order to gather attendance slips. Parents do not have to break in upon a teacher and class because they are "out of Church early today" and want their youngster for "an early start to the cottage.") Are children registered and introduced to their classes in such a way as to leave their classroom morale intact, or does the teacher inherit the results of introductory mishandling?

The tragedy of too many programs we dignify glibly with the name of "Church school" is that we have never provided the conditions of time, space, personnel recruitments, and job description which would let us make a really valid experiment with any curriculum. The provision of these conditions is the work of the administrator.

Our final responsibility to curriculum use is the most searching. Indeed, one suspects that few responsibilities in the parish are evaded more consistently than evaluation. Perhaps this is because evaluation is inevitably a process that includes us and our own Church school investment. Still, without evaluation we are like riflemen who shoot repeatedly without checking their targets.

Obviously, we cannot tell how well a given curriculum has worked unless we are clear about what we wanted from it in the first place. We have already nominated some possible standards: (1) Does it teach the faith? (2) Is it administratively practical? (3) Can our teachers use it? (4) Do our students learn from it?

Besides goal clarity, a second precondition for evaluation is just treatment for the people whose work is under scrutiny. It seems only fair that the groups who use the curriculum should have a part in designing its evaluation. (After all, without them, no recommendations can take real effect.)

Once our goals are understood, and the people involved in the process are respected, we are ready for the curriculum evaluation itself. It might well be organized around three questions.

First, we might ask, "Have we tried to make our curriculum work?" This first question really involves preconditions.

It should, therefore, first be put to the parish at large, parents, and administrators.

When the teacher's turn comes, a self-rating questionnaire is valuable. (It is, indeed, valuable for the teacher's work whether or not he turns it in.) Such a questionnaire might look like this: Did I understand the over-all goal and basic approach of my course? Did I familiarize myself with the organization of the manual's resources so that they were available for my week by week use? Did I begin thinking about my lesson plan early enough so that there would be time for reflection and development before the "final draft"? Did I evaluate my class work week by week with my team mate, and, on occasion, the class, or am I building my evaluation from the fragile memories of a whole year's work?

A second question to make up our evaluation might well be, "How much help did the curriculum give?" Here the questions already taken up in connection with curriculum choice might be in order.

A third and final question could be worded, "How did our Church school turn out with this particular curriculum?" Some of the things which make up success may be hard to get at in any tangible way. How does one chart "spiritual growth," for instance? Other factors can be looked into more objectively: For example, have the learners absorbed the required information? (If the course is concerned to teach the Ten Commandments, do the children now know them?) How does our attendance compare with that inspired by our old curriculum? Would questionnaires sent to parents, teachers, and students nominate it for another year's use?

Questions in appraisal of a given Church school may vary considerably from these. The important thing is that they come. The unexamined Church school life is not worth living, let alone re-living.

PART II
Educational Institutions

5

THE PARISH SCHOOL MOVEMENT: AN APPRAISAL

BY *John T. Russell*

THE PARISH day school (PDS) movement is a post-World War II phenomenon. To many perceptive people in the Church the Supreme Court decision in the McCollum Case (1947) demanded a re-thinking of the Church's responsibility for the whole education of her children. The McCollum Case (which forbade the use of public school property for optional religious instruction) was the beginning of a series of Court decisions which have withdrawn the public schools from their original conscious determination to assist in the nurture of Christian faith and morality. In our pluralistic society such decisions seem equitable to safeguard the rights of minorities. But a growing number of concerned Churchmen have asked themselves if true education can be divorced from conscious reference to Him who is the source of all truth and wisdom and from presuppositions about faith and the meaning of life which are axiomatic for Christians. The responses to this self-questioning have been varied.

Public Education

There has always been and there is probably now a general satisfaction and contentment with the public school system on the part of the great majority of Episcopalians. Multitudes of devoted Church people are intimately involved in public school education and they feel little perturbation over the recent radical secularization of the public schools. They fail to see that the omission of a perfunctory morning prayer and Bible verse makes any difference in the nurture of their children—and in this they are right. But they also believe that religion and faith can very well be confined to the provinces of the home and the Church. They fail to see that the basis of Christian criticism of present-day secular education is philosophical and metaphysical. This is, of course, understandable, since only a small minority of working educators have any conscious understanding of the several current philosophies of education that shape the methods and goals of public education. Nevertheless, our public education system is permeated by philosophical assumptions that are inimical to the Christian faith because they necessarily exclude consideration of faith and religion which alone provide that synthesis of disparate truths which illumines all knowledge with meaning for life and commitment.

The prevalent philosophical assumptions which hold the field in public education are there, not because they are the most reputable or defensible, but because the necessarily strict "neutrality" of the public system automatically excludes realistic philosophies of education. The public system accepts responsibility only for proximate goals and values (health, good citizenship, etc.) and officially abandons concern for more ultimate values. Nevertheless, the communication of values—overt or otherwise—proceeds throughout the formative years of education. The church and the home may preach. The school communicates by assumptions. The latter method is the more effective one.

The legally necessary dichotomy of truth into secular and sacred contradicts that most essential axiom that "truth is one," which itself is a corollary of the first biblical creed (the *Shema*), "Hear, O Israel, the Lord thy God is one. . . ." Any attempt to compartmentalize life or truth into sacred and secular is bound to be disastrous in the formation of integrated personalities. It is impossible to separate truth from values and any legal pretense to assume that crucial values are non-existent is itself a value assumption. The Christian Church has no quarrel with true secularism or true humanism, for these are concerned with the issues of existence in this *saeculum*, this age, this world—as is the biblical prophetical faith. But a radical secularism that avoids the Ultimate One who is the source of human freedom and historical concern leaves man prey to other demonic gods— racism, nationalism, selfism, nihilism.

The protection of minority rights in public education has resulted in a great loss of academic freedom, since only certain "values"—which are neither ultimate nor absolute— may be recognized. There is a veto on any attempt to relate or integrate truth by any reference to man's ultimate concern. This "neutrality" results in *de facto* recognition of positivism and the linguistic analysts' contention of the meaninglessness of theological propositions. The strict "neutrality" of the system becomes unintentionally hostile to faith by its legal inability to recognize ultimate values which alone can integrate the fragmented educational process with compelling conceptions or anything like a *Weltanschauung*. Most students would conclude from such silence that there are no ultimate values and that all values are relative.

It is difficult to see how the above state of affairs in public education can be avoided. (L. B. Whittemore in his penetrating book, *The Church and Secular Education*,[1] offers solutions for modification of the public system that would require the aroused conscience of the religious population to effect.) There are other defects in the public system which are legally avoidable, but which are too often prevalent. There is an appalling ignorance of the Bible and the basic *corpus* of religious knowledge. This profoundly affects any attempt to understand the basis of Western culture. Literature, history, philosophy—all the humanities—are enigmatic without theological foundations. Science itself, ". . . the inexpugnable belief that every detailed occurrence can be correlated with its antecedents in a perfectly definite manner, exemplifying general principles," has one source, ". . . the medieval insistence on the rationality of God."[2]

The Parish Day School Solution

The PDS movement is but one attempt at a solution to the problem of making education, and therefore life, meaningful and integrated. One obvious alternative is for the home and the Church to provide thorough instruction in the *corpus* of Christian knowledge together with a Christian *milieu* which can counteract the radical secularism of the public system. Those who lead the PDS movement are often disillusioned with the possibilities of satisfactory achievement either through home or Sunday school instruction. Many of them, influenced by the insight of the Liturgical Movement, would prefer Sunday to be devoted primarily to worship and the proclamation of the *kerygma*—the *didache* being communicated in the regular school week. (Such an ideal situation practically does not exist since all parishes must make provision for Sunday school instruction for those who do not attend the parish day school.) Various forms of a released time plan from the public schools have been advocated by responsible educators, but most of them demand the cooperation and interest of the whole religious community and to the continued dichotomization of education is added the disruption of normal school schedules. Many parishes have adopted the more radical solution of the PDS, not because it is an ideal solution, but because it is at least feasible.

The steady growth of the PDS movement during the past eighteen years is remarkable because it has flourished with very little encouragement from the hierarchy and the official educators of the Church. (Exactly the opposite was the situation at the beginning of the Roman Catholic parochial school movement.) It has flourished among a people who are traditionally staunch defenders of public education. Even today there is great ambivalence in the attitudes of Church officialdom concerning parish schools. While there is a recognition of the truth of much that has been said above, there is also an appreciation of something of the vast problem involved in such a venture. Some of the problems are merely theoretical; most of them are immensely practical.

The most common theoretical questions are: Are such separate schools consonant with our democratic way of life? Are such schools divisive? Aren't the Roman Catholics themselves reconsidering the advisability of parochial schools? It is strange for pure reasons of social theory that the first question should be asked. The peculiar glory of the American democratic theory is that it is not a monolithic society of conformity where the *vox populi vox dei* concept prevails, but a pluralistic society in which diversity is welcomed for the good of the whole. In the nineteenth century the non-Roman Catholic churches *voluntarily* relinquished the education of their children to the state when Horace Mann urged the adoption of a system modeled on the Prussian public schools. They were satisfied that Christianity would never be divorced from the schools of a Christian nation. (The McGuffey Readers were more than ample reassurance for decades.) These churches are perfectly free in our pluralistic society to assume again responsibility for the education of their young.

It is strange for the heirs of apostles and martyrs to worry about the divisiveness of Christian institutions. The reconciliation of all things in Christ can only proceed with the prior non-conformity to the world by Christians, for the secular standards and values and presuppositions, ignoring the spiritual life of man, are productive of alienation. It is true that parish schools could foster an unhealthy divisiveness if they were primarily instruments of sectarian culture with attendant narrowness and obscurantism and creative of a cultic pride disruptive to the larger Christian community. This is unlikely to be the case with Episcopal parish schools because of the comprehensive, non-confessional nature of Anglicanism. Few of our schools have been founded with a narrow churchmanship bias. It is not a concern for narrow churchmanship that makes a school flourish; it is a vital concern with *education*.

Mary Perkins Ryan in 1964 provoked much questioning in her widely-read book, *Are Parochial Schools the Answer?* [3] Mrs. Ryan, of course, dealt only with the gigantic Roman Catholic school system and much of her criticism is applicable only to that system with its built-in "siege mentality" (her phrase) against first the Protestant sectarian ethos at one time dominant in public schools and later against the onslaughts of such aspects of the modern Enlightenment which were not yet congenial to Rome. The spirit of Vatican II is already changing that mentality. Faced with the tremendous practical problems of maintaining this system, Mrs.

Ryan advocates a gradual closing of such schools in order to use its financial resources and manpower in other critical areas, such as the Latin American mission field. (Involved are more than $100,000,000 annually just for operation and maintenance, not new construction, and 103,000 sisters, 5,000 brothers, 13,000 priests—to say nothing of the lay teachers.) Convinced that full-time education is only an "auxiliary service" of the Church she proposes that the task of the Christian formation of persons be shifted to an intensified participation in the worship of the Church, augmented by out-of-school instruction in families and classes. The furor caused by her book has already subsided and Roman Catholic educators are proceeding with a further expansion of the parochial school system. There is no visible evidence for the rumor that ". . . the Roman Catholics are themselves disillusioned with parochial schools."

(The PDS movement has a common goal with the Roman Catholic school system—the Christian formation of children. But the PDS movement—purposely avoiding the term "parochial school" because of its Roman connotations—has no design of becoming a smaller version of the Roman Catholic system. The canonical control of education by the local rector decrees that our schools shall remain decentralized and voluntary and that there shall be great freedom in curriculum and educational experimentation. We are inclined to believe that local, involved educational authorities are as effective in making educational decisions as those in control in any centralized system, public or churchly. Our concern tends to be simply with education and less with cultic indoctrination.)

Practical Problems

The primary practical problem for the PDS is that of logistics. Where can the ordinary parish possibly find the physical facilities, manpower, and finances for such a venture? The problem becomes more acute each year as more federal aid for education makes larger the disparity between the financial resources of parish schools and public schools. The problem of facilities is the less serious. A large proportion of our parishes have magnificent educational facilities that are often used only for Sunday school. Simple modification and the addition of playground facilities are often more than sufficient for the efficient operation of a day school. The daily use of parish buildings is consonant with good stewardship.

The problem of manpower is more serious. We have no reservoir of religious (members of monastic orders) such as Rome possesses. Despite the magnificent job in education done by Episcopalian monks and nuns, most of our orders show no dominant interest in *parish* schools. Their own logistical problems tend to confine their attention to Church-related, independent schools owned by their own orders and often and necessarily geared for the affluent. Yet the Episcopal Church has a constituency of highly-educated and capable persons who are generous towards God and who are eager to serve Him with whatever talents they possess. There is nowhere that this immense reservoir of potential skill can be more readily drawn upon than in a parish situation. Involved parishioners can often fulfill all the auxiliary roles (secretaries, treasurers, gardeners, painters, housekeepers, art, language, and music teachers) in a highly competent manner. Multitudes of highly qualified teachers are eager to work for the Church's mission at considerable financial sacrifice.

The most serious practical objection to the PDS movement is the question of finance. Parish schools in affluent communities have little difficulty in charging sufficient tuition to enable them to match the salary scales of public schools.

Parish schools located in working class communities must often limit tuition rates to as little as twenty dollars per month—which still means considerable financial sacrifice to the parents, the teachers, and the parish. Understandably many Churchmen feel a guilty shock when they discover that many of our most effective and competent PDS teachers work for less than two hundred and fifty dollars per month. There are Churchmen who question the moral right of the Church to expect such sacrifices from its employees. The situation is compounded by the general lack of pension plans for these teachers other than their reduced Social Security benefits.

The financial problems of the PDS might not be a serious problem if the Church at large accepted the PDS as a normal function of a normal parish. Rare is the parish which, having a day school, is unanimous in its support by enrolling all their children and fully supporting the cost of the school. Since the PDS movement is young, many of its leaders believe that the Church will in time be converted to the movement and furnish proper support. In the meantime these severe financial sacrifices will continue because the teachers are motivated by a moral concern about education and the Christian faith that will not quit. In some places the financial crisis has been alleviated by munificent benefactors, but the real benefactors of the movement largely consist of those teachers who perform superior work for sub-standard wages.

A very practical question may be asked about parish day schools: "Are they as good as public schools academically?" This is a crucial question. The common feeling of the leaders of the movement is that a PDS must be academically superior to the public facilities of their community. A large percentage of our schools are striking examples of superior education. The Church must equip itself with canonical means to prevent the existence of inferior schools using the Church's name or property. In the Diocese of South Florida in 1965, a simple canon, giving authority to the Bishop and Executive Board to license, visit, accredit, and close PDS's, was unanimously adopted. The Department of Parish Day Schools advises the Bishop and Executive Board in these matters.

In the early years of the movement some tactical errors were made. Some schools felt obligated to accept some students with academic or emotional difficulties. This was a grave error which worked to the detriment of both the schools and the exceptional child. Children with academic and emotional problems need teachers specially trained for such work. There is a vast need in several parts of the country for the Church to sponsor such specialized schools, for the task cannot be done in a regular parish day school. All entering pupils must be tested and placed in grades according to their achievement level. The achievement test requirements, for instance, of the Florida Episcopal School Association are well above those of the State school system.

If the philosophical principles of education of the PDS movement are sound and our schools have competent teachers, there is no reason for PDS education to be anything but academically superior. Almost all our classes are small. We have an enviable freedom to utilize new techniques and curricula. Some of our schools, for instance, produce astounding results in teaching first-graders to read with the Initial Training Alphabet. Some use systems like the Cuisenaire Method in mathematics, the Carden Method, etc. Our teachers revel in this kind of "academic freedom" that is unrestricted by official red tape and is judged, not by its conformity to official routine, but solely by effective results. Most PDS's teach a foreign language in the elementary grades. Study of the Bible and the Christian faith assures a real foundation for the study of Western civilization and culture.

It is often necessary to remind interested people that the primary and almost sole function of the PDS is *education*. The Church as a whole has other concerns—evangelism, stewardship, social relations—and these concerns are shared by PDS Churchmen, but the Church's school is in trouble when it allows itself to forget its *raison d'être*, education. The school is not a vehicle for proselytizing students. Most of our schools have a respectable enrollment of children from non-Episcopalian families, but aside from expected conformity to the school's full schedule of study and worship there is no conscious effort to make Episcopalians of one and all. Most parishes with schools do receive considerable numbers of families whose first contact with the Church was through the school, but they were attracted primarily because of the Church's evident concern for education.

In questioning seminary graduates in their canonical examinations I was delighted to discover that they knew that the PDS movement stemmed from a series of Supreme Court decisions. My delight turned to shock when I detected that they meant, not the McCollum Case and its successors, but the decisions on school desegregation. Alas, there must be a segment of Church people who have made the facile assumption that the PDS movement is an attempt to secure private, racially segregated education. "After all," they said, "the movement is quite strong in the South." Such an inference must be frankly faced. The centers of strength in the PDS movement in the South were well established years before there was any real practical action towards the desegregation of the public school system. Although there is no practical way of assessing the racial views of patrons of PDS's, it is hardly reasonable to suppose that their dominant interest was in anything other than education, since no "threat" of integration really existed in the public system and since most of them were Church members. The ultimate impetus for the establishment of the PDS lies in the concern of the rectors of the various parishes. It is ignoble to assume that priests would be willing to complicate their time and ministry in order to deny or frustrate the clear teaching of the Church in regard to racial prejudice. Many Southern PDS's took deliberate steps to assure racial integration of their schools before public school integration was realized. Some of them received financial help from the Church's Executive Council when a reduced enrollment resulted. One renowned school in the South—not really a parish school— was forced to sever its connection with the Church because of its discriminatory policies. Many other schools are not integrated precisely because they are *parish* day schools ministering to people within their parish bounds and for child-centered educational reasons they do not seek to transport children of another race miles every day to achieve a result which is merely exhausting for the child and which has dubious value in the social revolution. I know of no PDS's which have racially discriminatory policies and I believe that such a policy would bar its use of the Church's name. But the fact that there is *any* school which is not racially mixed is disturbing to some high-minded critics of the movement. The PDS must always be primarily and almost solely concerned with education. The educator has an arduous task, a task which he believes, when well done, will best contribute to the transformation of the world. As Gilbert Highet says concerning the educator and the social revolution, "He has done his full share. Let others do theirs." [4] The PDS movement is not an attempt to avoid integration. It does what is reasonably possible in the Christian social revolution, for education, like politics, is the art of the possible.

Growth of the Movement

The centers of strength of the movement are in the Provinces of Sewanee, the Southwest, Washington, and the Pacific. The states of Texas, Florida, California, New York, and Maryland, and the District of Columbia advanced in numbers of schools and enrollment. In most cases these centers of strength developed through the powerful leadership of individual Churchmen who pioneered the movement in widely separated areas. The movement has been growing out geographically from these centers of successful education. People have to see the success of the PDS to be inspired to such an undertaking in their own parishes. It is a "grass roots" movement. Approximately five thousand teachers are already employed in the PDS movement. This means there are already about half as many teachers in this churchly vocation as there are ordained clergy in our Church. There are already more than five hundred strictly *parish* day schools in the continental United States alone, and more than fifty more in our overseas missions. State-wide Episcopal School Associations have been formed in Louisiana and Texas. The pioneer Florida Episcopal School Association in 1965 became a South Florida organization with the withdrawal of the Diocese of Florida to function under a diocesan Board of Regents.

(It is interesting to note that other non-Roman Catholic parish schools have geographical centers of strength also in this country. Almost half of all Lutheran schools are in the Great Lakes area; the main center of strength for Seventh Day Adventist schools is California; almost half of the Christian Reformed schools are in Michigan; half of all Friends' schools are in Pennsylvania. The Episcopal Church's PDS movement is unusual in that its centers of strength are not determined by the comparative population density of Episcopalians.)[5]

The national Episcopal Parish School Association, founded at Washington in 1949, became the Division for Parish and Day Schools of the Episcopal School Association (which also included divisions for non-parochial and boarding schools) in 1954. The first national conference of Episcopal Schools was held at Washington in 1960, followed in 1963 by the second Washington Conference. In May of 1965 the name of the association was changed to the National Association of Episcopal Schools. The Rev. Dr. Clarence W. Brickman, Associate Secretary for Parish and Preparatory Schools of the national Church's Department of Christian Education, and long a leader in the movement, retired at the end of 1964. The new Executive Secretary of the National Association, the Rev. John P. Carter, will not be an officer of the Executive Council of the national Church.

The PDS movement is young. About half of its schools are now only kindergartens. (Most parishes begin with a Kindergarten and add a grade a year.) Its growth has been consistent for the past 18 years, and this growth will probably continue, regardless of its logistics problem. It represents a radical attempt at the parish level to deal with the problem of Christian education. It is not a wholly satisfactory answer (is there any?), because it is a rare parish that can enroll all its children in the PDS. It demands an extraordinary amount of time, energy, and commitment from rectors, teachers, parents, and parishioners. Yet some believe that nowhere else can the Church have a more intimate and intensive impact on the formative years of her children.

6

CHRISTIAN
EDUCATION IN
CHURCH-RELATED
AND INDEPENDENT
SCHOOLS

BY *Allen F. Bray, III*

A T THIS writing there are more than seven hundred schools below the college level either owned by, or affiliated with, the Episcopal Church. Immediately involved in Christian education in this context are more than seventy thousand students, their teachers, parents, and the various staffs and boards of the schools they attend. Within the past fifteen years, the number of Church-related schools has doubled. This and the added factor of the increased vitality of such resource agencies as the Unit of Parish and Preparatory Schools of the Department of Christian Education of the Executive Council, and both the regional and national Episcopal Schools Associations testify to the importance of this area of the Church's life.

The relationship of the Christian Church to education is no new development; neither is the concern of the Episcopal Church for the work of the schools at the various levels of the educational process. The determination on the part of parents for the Christian education of their young in a formal structure created for that purpose somewhat parallels the development of the Sunday schools. It is also similar in the sense that the founding principle has not always been maintained in the reality of practice. In many cases the Church schools provided a more advanced opportunity for cultural education with closer attention and supervision than could be given in the public schools. The originally distinctive element of Christian education soon became, in many cases, merely accepted as part of the "seasoning," a sort of to-be-expected by-product of the combination of the place and the process.

This trend, however, shows evidences of being reversed as the schools re-think their basic mission and the individuals in the schools reconsider the nature and responsibilities of their Christian discipleship. The school founded out of concern for, and/or dedicated to, the task of Christian education expresses its significant difference not merely in the maintenance of a hallowed tradition, nor in the customary ecclesiastical expressions at the appropriate times, nor in a stated relationship or sponsorship. It is not simply *a* school in relation to or competition with other schools. Neither is it *a* school differing merely in certain requirements and, for its tuition, offering certain additional facilities and special programs. It is a school in which, according to Dr. William Hogue, academic excellence is viewed as a theological imperative. Achievement of this ideal is contingent upon many factors, not the least of which are the following.

The Church and the School

First, perhaps one of the greatest barriers to both the Church-related and the independent schools, and one which must be overcome, is the barrier of pseudo-identification; *i.e.*, the structure of relationship and responsibility either within or without the framework of the institutional church. Tradition and form may provide the structure for apparent meaning and necessary incentive. They can also serve as major obstacles, however, and to this truth the New Testament bears abundant witness. On the other hand, the independent school, free of any formal ties of ecclesiastical relationship, can so shy from the indications or implications of Christian commitment that it denies by omission and betrays by neglect the religious trust and need of its individual members.

Second, possibly the greatest opportunity for the Church in the schools of today lies in the recognition that obedient service and faithful witness are not determined by what is printed on a brochure or in a certificate of membership or affiliation, but by personal and corporate commitment to the truth of God made known in Jesus Christ and proclaimed through the abiding power of His Holy Spirit. Recognition of this results in a contemporary boldness of definition reminiscent of the early Church. One school of fairly recent origin, for example, defines its purpose in a most unusual way in the opening paragraph of its brochure: "Its basic purpose is to proclaim the good news that Jesus Christ, who was crucified, is risen and that through faith in Him all men may become partakers now of everlasting life. Its purpose, therefore, is the same as that of the Church." [1]

Third, if one understands the Church as the *ecclesia,* the people of God, it follows that wherever the people are, there is the Church, declared in the legal sense or not. Christian education in the schools, then, is not so much a matter of "official" relationship as it is a matter for the personal stewardship of the gifts of talent and opportunity which have been entrusted to each of us. The mission of the Church, at least as far as Christian education is concerned, is not always or only accomplished in a given building at designated holy hours, or in specific classrooms with specific instructors. The fundamental truth of God for education is that the limited term, "sacred studies," is both irrelevant and irreverent; all studies are sacred or no studies are sacred.

Fourth, granted that Western culture as we know it has a double rootage, with one foot in the Hebraic and one foot in the Hellenic. Granted that this dichotomy is more apparent and more significant for our daily lives than we often realize because it is so tacitly accepted. Granted that this dual rootage accounts for much of our fragmentation and certainly that significant portion of it which so easily accepts the heresy that "religion is a part of life," implying that there are other "parts," co-equal, co-substantial, and co-eternal.

Yet the work of the Christian involved in the culture—and no Christian is uninvolved—is not to renounce the culture but to redeem it. Education is the means by which the culture is transmitted, and Christian education views the aspirations and the activities of a given culture within the perspective of a greater purpose than that provided by a limited national or ethnic vision. In a sense Christian education is the destroyer of the cultural barrier, for it speaks to the oneness of creation and its Creator, unifying the facets in the meaningfulness of His eternity and rescuing them from the abyss of a mechanistic meaninglessness. The difference between cultural and Christian education—a prime distinction for the work of the Church in the schools—is aptly described by Iris V. Cully:

> Cultural education is anthropocentric; the education of the church is theocentric. Yet each has a witness to make to the other. Cultural education reminds men of their value as human beings and of their potential accomplishments. It

will stress the enrichment made by science and aesthetics in those times when some people within the church fail to appreciate these gifts to mankind. The church, by acknowledging God as the center of all existence, can keep men from the distortions of life that come when they make themselves as gods.[2]

Thus, as the instrument of the Church, as one of its missionary enterprises, the school must recognize and relate to the fullness of the demands, the dangers, and the delights of human life as men and women, boys and girls, know and experience it. Christian education in the schools must confront this cultural complexity with the comprehensive firmness of a faith which realistically and patiently awaits fulfillment in a time and at a season appropriate to its Author. This is not so much a matter of stated school policy as it is of individual practice and profession. It is approached and accomplished individually, through the miracle of personal conversion which, in turn, becomes the catalyst by which all things are made new in the acknowledgment of their shared foundation and sharing relationship. Although it is necessary in all vocations, it is imperative in the schools that we understand that not merely the assigned function, but the fullness of responsible, faithful citizenship at all times and in all places is the means by which the boundaries are crossed and the high calling is accomplished.

In both the Church-related and the independent schools, the work of the Church is the same, although it may be more clearly defined and more obviously structured in the former than in the latter. Form and structure, however, are neither as significant nor as conducive to acceptance as is the witness of the committed Christian, be that person headmaster, chaplain, instructor in physics, janitor of the recreation building, or nurse.

Therefore in any and in all of its members the Church is at work in the world, in the schools and their chapels, their classrooms, playing fields, dormitories and dining halls. These are the testing grounds of the faith as received and observed. These are the arenas and activities in which the children live their lives and work out their respective pilgrimages to a maturity which is, we trust, as fully spiritual as it is physical, emotional, and intellectual. It is a testimony to the truth that there is nowhere where God is not. It is proof of the power of *koinonia,* that blessed community "in which both men and God participate in an intricate web of relationships." [3] It is a community of power and of purpose, a community of learning and of loving.

Whether the task be approached from the standpoint of a stated relationship to a denominational body or in the freedom of stipulated independence, opportunities for the schools in which Christian education is recognized as a concomitant are provocatively and realistically set forth in the following statement by G. E. Jackson:

> Reality, it seems to me, consists in learning how to live, which includes all personal relations; to worship, which involves man in ultimate concern; to work, which is man's creative endeavor; to play, which is man's right to full pleasure; and to die, which is man's confession of his own finitude. Christian education is that process by which each is helped to live more fully in terms of at least these five aspects of reality. To *think* theologically then really means to *do* theologically: to love one another, to worship God, to let the work of our hands be creatively used by God in his service, to learn to enjoy fully the present moment as we make full use of our leisure, and to die not heroically nor stoically but trusting him who is beyond our finitude.[4]

The schools of the Church and the Church in the schools are aware of this imperative. They are aware, too, of the mood of sophisticated skepticism which has seduced many of our youngsters because they have seen the betrayal of many standards on many sides. They are aware of the pessimism which permeates many who have been reared in the shade of the mushroom-shaped cloud. They know the pace of activities and the volume of noise are but symptoms of an insecurity that dares not confront itself in the quietude of solitude. Therefore, on this ground, they face the realities of their commitment to Christ in the midst of the confusion of the contemporary culture. In conversations with school people one is made aware of the serious questions which are being searchingly asked of them by students and, consequently, by the school people of themselves.

In the schools today there are increasingly honest efforts which take a variety of forms to explore and evaluate the old and new avenues of communication and dedication to both the Fount of Wisdom and to those who, in this time and in their tender years bear His image. This awareness on the part of faculties and staffs is reflected in the atmosphere of contagion which exists between the good teacher and the well-taught, in the hunger so often obtusely expressed by the young and compassionately recognized by the perceptive instructor. This is an awareness, however, which must be communicated to and permeate the *ecclesia* as a whole, for surely the burdens of one another are some of the joys of discipleship. As Findley Edge pointed out, "If the church is a company of persons who have been called by God to continue the ministry of Jesus in the contemporary world, then each member of that company has a distinct responsibility for ministry." [5]

A Trinity of Reality

To appreciate the task and the challenge of Christian education in the schools one must be aware that a Christian philosophy of education is inextricably bound up with the Christian doctrine of man and is, of faithful necessity, as comprehensive, admitting and speaking not only to his actuality but to his aspiration. There is, then, a pragmatism to Christian education which can be viewed as a trinity of reality. The first member of that trinity is God, the Creator of all worlds, the Father of all life, the Redeemer of all brokenness and the Sanctifier of all aspiration. The knowledge of God as real and as Reality is the foundation-stone of Christian education. Without or apart from this, our researches and our thought systems are but vanities, serving no lasting purpose and providing at best but partial illumination for a limited time. When in the course of our quest for truth and understanding, our separated vanity challenges the actuality or the intention of the mystery, the fullness of Reality speaks to us even as to Job: "Who is this that darkens counsel by words without knowledge? Gird up your loins like a man, I will question you, and you shall declare to me" (Job 38: 2-3, RSV).

The communication and acceptance of the Reality, then, is cardinal in the educational effort, in the variety of the revelatory activity. Both the fullness of present and past experience as well as the abundance of potential encounter provide the substance in and through which there come knowledge, acceptance, and response, sufficient to the needs as they arise. Content, curriculum, time, and place are important, but personal witness more than methodology, freedom in faithful stewardship more than formalism in communication, contribute toward the accomplishment of this intended purpose and illustrate its relevance to all times and places.

Inasmuch, then, as the source of all creativity is God, the beginning, as Randolph Crump Miller has signified, must be in and with Him.

The proper starting point of Christian education is to face up to the challenge of the meaning of Christ, to discover what faith in Jesus Christ as Lord and Savior actually implies in terms of today's problems of living, and to be sure of the truth of the conclusions reached. To avoid this central question of Christian faith, as some writers of lesson materials and teachers, parents, and pastors have done, means enfeebling the educational system of the Church at its very heart.[6]

The second member of the trinity of reality is the world in which we live, rich with its natural resources for both spiritual and material depth and dilemma, often poverty-stricken in its use of those resources to meet the opportunities, the challenges, and the changes of the time. Christianity is not a religion *of* the world, but it is definitely *in* the world and, hopefully, as the leaven in the dough, not condemning, but calling to recognition, repentance, and redemption. This, then, means that a part of our task as Christian educators in the schools is to know and communicate the fullness of our world, its cultures, conditions, and constitution.

The Christian is not in opposition to the world, for it is God's creation. He or she does, however, measure this world with the measure of Christ, in order that all things may be stimulated to grow unto the stature and the fullness intended by Him. The relation of the Church to the world—and this is primarily a one-to-one relationship of person to situation—needs continually to be re-examined and seen in the richness of its reality. Christian education in the school exists not to provide a quasi-ghetto or a religio-cultural island in the form of a school but a base of operations for the extension and the implementation of God's truth and response and purpose through the lives and works of its individual members.

It has been said many times in many ways, but it bears

repetition: the truth that is the concern of education is both immediately and ultimately the concern of society. The meaning of what is or is not taught is related to the experience quotient of the individual student. Christian education, thus, is education about life in the light of God, for life in the service of God. It is as concerned with the present as with the future and values the past as resource and preparation. Much, therefore, of what is designated as Christian education takes place outside the structured class and finds its fulfillment in such often unexpected existential encounters.

The third aspect of the trinity of reality in a pragmatic philosophy of Christian education is the relationship between the Alpha and Omega of all that is and the world in which the witness is presently borne. This relationship is individualized in the persons who walk in this world by the light of Him who said, "I am the way, the truth, and the life." The mission is strikingly defined in the title of a recent book which gives an account of one area of missionary activity, *God's Colony in Man's World.*[7]

The locus of the action and the interaction between God and the world is the human personality. Preparation for this work and the accomplishment of this witness is the high task of the schools. Much has been said to our youngsters about the privileges and responsibilities of citizenship. For Christian education in the schools, however, citizenship is of a dual type: in this world and, as St. Paul said, "in heaven." The duties and demands require a strong foundation for decision, for it is at such a moment that effective witness is borne. Reamer Kline once said, "The place of supreme importance for witness in every age, is the place of decision." The developing life is that place of a certainty, and in its questing and probing, in its response and reaction, decisions of varying degrees of importance would appear to be the one constant in the midst of flux. The importance of the interaction between God and His world, and the place of the person as the scene of the activity cannot be under-estimated. As Daniel D. Williams wrote: "All Christian education should be either preparation for decision or confrontation with it. The meaning of faith does not become clear until one has made his personal decision, and has begun to participate in the reality of the story of sin and grace as his own story." [8]

To prepare the students for such participation is the solemn responsibility of our schools and the function of Christian education in any and all of its forms. The schools of the Church and the representatives of the Church in the schools are much aware of the demands which are placed upon youngsters in and by the contemporary culture. Because they are also concerned for the faithful and relevant communication of the reality of God to this time of testing, old forms and new are being tested and evaluated in an attempt to discover more effective means and methods of presentation. A dynamic spirit recognizes the variance of both methodology and approach within the structure of content and dares to explore and experiment in at least three prime areas of the life of the schools: their worship, their religious studies, and the general ethos of the school.

School and Chapel

The so-called Church-related schools have long been characterized by what is unfortunately known as "required" chapel. The very phrase points up the existence of the dichotomy referred to earlier and thereby contributes to a disservice and a dissatisfaction. One seldom hears of "required" English or "required" algebra. Students, faculty, and parents accept the necessity for instruction in these areas as a normative part of the educational process and regard regular attendance at such classes as an expected part of the educational process. The concern as to whether or not one "is made" to attend chapel is reflective of the separateness and the disparity between the philosophy and the practice of Christian education.

To counteract this and have the relevance of the worship experience clearly understood in relation to the full reality of life as it is lived and experienced both with and without God, numerous schools are departing from the traditional routine of rigidly scheduled and routinely conducted services. They are attempting to provide services of varying types which are both integrative and inspiring, summing up and reflecting the totality of exposure and aspiration, the wealth of triumphs and tragedies which provide the fabric of the lives of the worshipping community.

Massey Shepherd has defined liturgy as "the quintessence of Christian education itself, the focus of its inspiration and its fulfillment." Surely implicit in this is the concept of both prayer and preaching as related to the needs of the people for and by whom they arise. They issue from a pastoral concern and connotes awareness of the series of individual and corporate relationships to the world as we know it and the Lord of history as He makes Himself known.

The discipline of regularity and constancy is positive. But this discipline borders on the irrelevant unless and until it finds itself as the channel through which flows the "good news" of God, addressing itself to the hearts and minds of those for whom it is intended. The worship life of the school, then, and the worshipping activity of its individual members, should relate the truth of God to the perceived needs of man in this time and this situation. It must address itself to the present moment from the resources of its faith in God's eternity, allowing for the quiet moment of individual introspection as well as the triumphal occasion of congregational praise and thanksgiving.

The area of religious studies, long regarded as a separate and distinct part of the curriculum would appear now to be qualified by a trend toward inclusion of the material in other areas of study such as music, art, language, literature, science, and mathematics. Inasmuch as faith informs all knowledge, and knowledge requires faith for its fulfillment, the boundaries of insight are slowly being lowered and interdisciplinary researches are no longer novel.

Although the marking-out of a particular area as deserving of special attention and treatment may have arisen from the best of intentions, from a practical point of view the establishment of "required" courses in religion singles them out as special and by fiat set in among or against what one school chaplain referred to as "the real courses." The distinction by definition and practice regardless of intention serves no good purpose and contributes to the extension of the cultural dichotomy rather than the development of religious understanding and the sense of discipleship as comprehensive. This is not to suggest justification for such an emasculated study as "The Bible as Literature." It is, to the contrary, to suggest that the riches of the Scripture are indeed great literature, but that what makes them so is their faith-fullness. Doubtless Faulkner could not be studied effectively without reference to the Southern culture which was the marrow of his bone and the moon of his creativity.

The use of laymen, convinced in the faith and skilled communicators in their respective academic disciplines not merely of knowledge but of God's truth, is one of the highest opportunities for the extension of the Church's ministry of Christian education in the schools. The truth of what Paul Vieth wrote some time ago is becoming even more apparent in the present generation: "One of the reasons that so many send their children to the church school is that these children may receive additional ethical guidance. But character education is one thing; Christian education is something more." [9] This "something more" is or is not reflected in the ethos—that ideal and universal element which characterizes and identifies the totality—of the school in particular and all the schools in which the living God is acknowledged to be present and served. It is revealed in the secure quietness as well as the strong joyfulness of the community. It is sensed in the attitude, experienced in the shared devotions and acknowledged in the personal-ness of the response both to situations and persons. There is, where this is present, an observable sense of service, a communicated satisfaction of belonging, and a demonstrated dedication to a purpose which sustains and fulfills. It is neither contained nor disavowed by buildings, ceremonies, or traditions. It is made manifest in ways as manifold as the stars, as minuscule as the unseen atom. Yet in all and each there is a testimony, a surety, and a promise which is sufficient for allegiance and an incitement to participation in the inspiration. This ethos is manifested in the individual who, in any capacity, participates in the school community and experiences increased personal and social understanding and service.

The schools in which the Church is to any degree present and participating are characterized more by a sense of quest, a dedication to greater faithfulness and more effective communication. Seminars and study groups, student activity in worship services, not so much as leaders but as participants, conferences within school communities, agencies which bring together students and faculties from several schools, prayer and Bible study groups, dialogues between and within disciplines—all these and other techniques are present experiments being conducted in a wide variety of circumstances, dedicated and designed solely to relate God to man and man to God more clearly and convincingly.

Christian education in the schools, then, is really no different in principle, in philosophy, from Christian education in any other area. Its charge and its joy are the same. Its task and its challenge are neither more nor less than in any other arena of life. In the schools, however, there is perhaps the greater and more specific opportunity to bridge the abyss, to restore the unity of the humanly imposed dichotomy, and thereby to bring into human life that oneness of purpose and effort which is not conformity but reverent commitment to the cause and the call of Him by whose love we were created and in whose will we find our peace.

7
CHURCH-RELATED COLLEGES

BY *Reamer Kline*

THE EPISCOPAL Church's record with colleges presents some sharp contrasts with that of some other major Christian communions in the United States.

The Church has a strong commitment to learning. Its early American leaders were Oxford or Cambridge educated. It has consistently been rigorous in requiring college education for its ministry. The Church has almost indisputably had a higher-than-average level of learning in both its clergy and its laity, and has in general held to a rather refined level of taste in liturgy, music, architecture, and church appointments. In most of the better known American colleges, young people of the Church have made up a larger proportion of the student body than one would have expected from the small percentage the Church constitutes in the general population. And Episcopalian philanthropy has bulked far larger in building up the resources of the more strongly established American colleges than would normally be expected from a religious communion which constitutes only two percent of the population.

And yet, in the face of this strong belief in higher education and deep involvement in it, the Episcopal Church has created and maintained fewer Church-related colleges

102

than any other major United States Christian communion. Why? Some reasons for this are suggested below.

Although the Episcopal Church has seemed to lag behind its sister communions in the number of its Church-related colleges, there is reason to believe that it may be ahead of some other bodies in its handling of those institutions, and in the place its colleges occupy in the total pattern of the country's intellectual life. Episcopalians, unlike other religious bodies, have not expressed their "college urge" by establishing a large number of colleges and then tying their colleges tightly into the denominational structure. Now, willingly or perforce, other denominations are abandoning their former "close control" concept for their colleges, having found it outdated and intellectually stultifying. In the resulting new climate, the Episcopal Church-related colleges are enjoying a new recognition of their significance and influence.

The Historical Development

To understand American church-related higher education and the Episcopal Church's place in it, it is necessary briefly to review the record of Church involvement in the founding of America's colleges, and then to consider specifically the Episcopal Church's role in this enterprise.

As soon as they had gained a precarious foothold on the shores of the New World, the first settlers turned to the creation of institutions of higher education. Harvard was founded within six years of the settlement of Boston. Because of the theocratic nature of the early settlements, and the fact that in most of them the ministers were the chief (and often the only) men of learning, the early colleges were "religion centered." "Education in colonial America was the child of religion." [1] To perpetuate the ministry was a large share of the early college's function: "One of the first things we longed for and looked after was to advance Learning and perpetuate it to Posterity dreading to leave an illiterate ministry to the Churches when our present ministers shall lie in the Dust." [2]

Religious bodies played a major part in the founding of the nine Colonial colleges,[3]—Harvard, 1636 (Congregational); William and Mary, 1693 (Episcopal); Yale, 1701 (Congregational); Princeton, 1746 (Presbyterian); Columbia (King's College), 1754 (Episcopal); Pennsylvania, 1755 (Episcopal); Brown, 1765 (Baptist); Rutgers, 1766 (Dutch Reformed); Dartmouth, 1769 (Congregational).[4]

All of the nine Colonial colleges broke away from the control of their founding religious bodies, beginning with Pennsylvania right after the Revolutionary War, and ending with Brown in 1942.

The great post-Colonial period of founding of Church-related colleges in the United States was the era of "the settlement of the West"—especially the half-century from 1815 to the end of the Civil War. (The Roman Catholic colleges are an exception, most of them dating from after the Civil War.) As on the Eastern seaboard in colonial times, so too in the Mid-West and the West, the churches took the lead in starting colleges because there were no other educational resources on the frontier, and the churches were the only organized bodies with interest and strength enough to do the job. (And as with Harvard two centuries before, there was also the special need of the churches to provide an educated ministry.)

Of the first 120 colleges founded in the country (from 1636 to 1850), about 100 were established under Church auspices.[5] By 1954, the *Educational Directory* was listing 751 four-year accredited liberal arts colleges in the United States, and of these, 441 were affiliated with some religious group.[6]

A recent study by the Danforth Foundation (1965) puts the number of United States collegiate institutions of all kinds at 2100, of which 817 are classified as "associated with religious bodies." [7]

Unlike the Colonial colleges, a substantial proportion of the Church-sponsored colleges of the Mid-West and the West have continued in relationship with their founding bodies. Today the roll of colleges acknowledging a Church relationship includes 102 Methodist colleges, 45 Presbyterian colleges, 30 Lutheran, 29 Southern Baptist, 28 Baptist, 21 Congregational, and 8 Episcopalian. A majority in all the groups except the Episcopalian are west of the Alleghenies. There are 339 Roman Catholic colleges, pretty generally distributed over the area east of the Mississippi, with a few farther west. The total impact of the Church-related college movement has led the former executive director of the American Association of Colleges to write: "The church and the four-year colleges have been the chief agencies responsible for the rapid rise of the United States to its prominence as a world power." [8] And the 1965 Danforth Foundation study reports that "some of the most productive institutions in the United States are church colleges." [9]

It would appear that the Episcopalians, having now only eight colleges, played a proportionally smaller part in the nineteenth-century Church-related college movement than they had in the establishment of the pre-Revolutionary Colonial colleges. The explanation lies partly in the pre-Revolutionary Anglicans' self-image of themselves as an "established Church"; partly in their disadvantaged position as "Tories" after the War; and partly in the fact that Episcopalians were less represented than some other denominations in the population groups that "migrated west" in the early nineteenth century.

The pre-Revolutionary Anglican Churchmen in America

had pictured higher education in Oxford-Cambridge terms, as a function of the "Establishment" of which they themselves were a part—often even the leaders. (Two-thirds of the signers of the Declaration of Independence were Episcopalians.) It did not occur to Anglicans in America to create educational institutions primarily to serve any special segment or sect in the population, nor did they think of themselves as being such a minority. Because of the nature of English society, the Anglican sponsorship of Oxford and Cambridge was in effect a sponsorship by the entire power structure of the nation. It took some time for it to become apparent that in the fragmented denominational pattern of nineteenth-century America, sponsorship of a college by a denominational group gave the "denominational college" a far narrower and more restricted role than that played by Oxford and Cambridge. As the tensions caused by what was in effect a narrow sectarian control came to be realized, many American colleges parted company with their denominational sponsors.

The Episcopal Church-related Colleges

There are eight fully-accredited four-year colleges which are related to the Episcopal Church by charter, history, or tradition.

The eight colleges and their dates of origin are:

Hobart College, Geneva, N.Y., 1822.

Trinity College, Hartford, Conn., 1823.

Kenyon College, Gambier, Ohio, 1824.

University of the South, Sewanee, Tenn., chartered 1857, opened 1868.

Bard College, Annandale-on-Hudson, N.Y., 1860 (known as St. Stephen's up to 1934).

St. Augustine's College, Raleigh, N.C., 1867.

St. Paul's College, Lawrenceville, Va., 1888.

Shimer College, Mount Carroll, Ill., Church relationship established 1959; the college dates from 1853.

These institutions were brought together in 1961 through the personal initiative of Presiding Bishop Arthur Lichtenberger, with the result that the colleges joined to establish the Foundation for Episcopal Colleges (subsequently renamed the Fund for Episcopal Colleges). The purposes of this organization are "to represent its member colleges before the Church and the nation, and to open for these colleges new possibilities for their academic enrichment." [10]

Present programs of the Episcopal-related institutions through this group enterprise include establishment of visiting professorships, faculty fellowships, distinguished lectureships in the member institutions, scholarship programs for Negroes and for young people from Episcopal parishes, exchange of students among the eight institutions, and programs for strengthening their libraries.

A significant aspect of these colleges is the degree to which as a group they reflect and embody some of the major movements and social forces of American history. One of the earliest (Trinity of Hartford) sprang from the efforts of Anglicans in the new Republic to create for themselves a cultural pattern free from Calvinist domination. Two of the colleges (Hobart and Kenyon) were founded as part of the movement to bring educational opportunity to the Western frontier. Two others (Bard and Sewanee) proceeded from the new vigor in American life which was contemporaneous with the Civil War (though not a result of that war). Two more (St. Paul's and St. Augustine's) grew out of the great post-Civil War effort to provide new opportunities in life for the recently freed Negroes. The Church-related status of

Shimer, the newest comer to the eight-college family, is a product of the post-World War II appreciation in the Church of the strategic importance of higher education in our American culture.

Of the eight institutions, four are for men only (Trinity, Hobart, Kenyon and Sewanee). Four are coeducational (Bard, Shimer, St. Paul's, and St. Augustine's).

There is no "all women's college" in the group (although William Smith, the women's affiliate of Hobart and nondenominational by stipulation of its founder, is in many ways "more Episcopalian" than some of the historically Church-related institutions).

All are "small colleges," ranging from 450 to 1050 students. The "Church-relatedness" of these institutions is expressed in several ways:

(a) In their production of clergy, particularly at Trinity, Hobart, Bard, and Sewanee (over six hundred each have come from Bard and from Hobart).

(b) Occasionally in a doctrinally based curriculum, as at Sewanee.[11]

(c) All have chapels in which the services are those of the Book of Common Prayer. The colleges differ as to whether chapel attendance is optional or at least in part required, but all the institutions stress the chapel as an integral part of their life. Four of the eight colleges have a stated requirement as to chapel attendance, and four state that it is voluntary or a matter of individual decision.

Only one of the eight institutions (Sewanee) is controlled (and in this instance also owned) by the Church or its constituent units—in this case by twenty-one Southern Dioceses. Only Sewanee, St. Paul's and St. Augustine's receive any significant portion of their support through Church budgets, national, diocesan, or parochial.

The eight colleges collectively have a total of sixty million dollars of endowment. However these resources are very unevenly distributed, forty-six million of the total being in the hands of two of the eight institutions. On the other hand, the four least affluent have among them a total of less than two million dollars of endowment.

The founders of America's small colleges—especially the older ones—generally felt that rural or small-town locations were to be preferred, as being free of distractions and "the temptations of the city." This fact is reflected in the location of the eight Episcopal Church-related institutions. Only two are in cities of so much as medium size (Trinity in Hartford and St. Augustine's in Raleigh); one (Hobart) is in a very small city; and the other five are in small towns or villages.

The Episcopal Church is unusual among strongly structured religious bodies in that it has allowed its colleges (and its preparatory schools) to be independent institutions. Unlike colleges of Methodist, Lutheran, or Presbyterian connection, the Episcopal Church-related institutions are not supervised by or accountable to any "Church Board of Education," nor to any religious order as are many Roman Catholic institutions. This has permitted the growth of greater academic freedom in these institutions than is characteristic of Church-related colleges generally. Episcopalian influence in the colleges having that ancestry has been largely in terms of history, tradition, atmosphere, and individual personal witness.

In addition to the eight colleges discussed above, there are three other institutions in varying forms of relationship to the Church:

Cuttington College and Divinity School, a missionary college re-established in Suakoko, Liberia in 1949, and having two hundred students in 1965.

Trinity College, Quezon City, Manila. Responsibility for

this institution was taken over in 1963 by the Philippine Episcopal Church and the Philippine Independent Church. In 1965 Trinity had 356 students in its college program.

St. Michael's College, which in 1965 was in process of organization as an Episcopal-related unit in a new cluster of colleges associated with the University of the Pacific, Stockton, Calif.

Finally, to complete the record from an historical standpoint, in addition to the Episcopal Church-related colleges and the Colonial colleges mentioned above, there have been at various times a total of forty-seven other institutions in the founding or early fostering of which the Episcopal Church played a major part. These institutions have either changed to completely secular status or have disappeared from the scene.

The Changing Situation

Two questions must be faced by Church-related colleges and by those concerned for these institutions' continued relevance and significance in our national life:

(a) Can they continue, and should they continue, as "special communities" of people who share definite beliefs and goals?

(b) What shall be the distinctive role of these colleges in twentieth-century American society?

The first question relates to the issue of particularism and generalism in American history and in our American society. Until quite recently the United States was in many ways a land of regional cultures, local ethnic groups, and many "islands" of specialized mores, religious allegiances, and languages or dialects. In such a national pattern, it was natural for religious denominations to establish institutions of all sorts (including educational institutions) which embodied the credal convictions, social patterns, and often even the language or "native dress" of their sponsoring communities. Such patterns did not seem to be an infringement on the freedoms or rights of choice of other people, for the simple reason that not many people espousing different ways of life came into the orbit of these institutions or sought admission to them. A "denominational college" for example, was pretty generally seen as serving the constituency of its own denomination, and an overwhelming percentage of its teachers and students would be either birthright members or sincere converts to its beliefs and practices.

But beginning right after World War II, a great new mobility and whole new pattern of mass communication became facts of American life. People who had been born or reared in ethnic communities began to consider themselves members of American society at large. What had previously been seen as an embodiment of particular ways, beliefs, or interests, began to be viewed as "discriminatory" or as an instrument of "prejudice." The First and Fourteenth Amendments to the Federal Constitution were increasingly cited against the use of race or religion as a consideration in assigning a person to any role, and against letting these facts constitute either a barrier or an advantage to him in determining where he should go or what he should be.

The McCollum Case of 1947 in Illinois produced the first of a long series of court rulings which increasingly removed religious considerations from educational policy and practice, initially in public institutions and subsequently in private ones.

During these same years, students of all backgrounds and beliefs were more and more seeking admission to what had formerly been considered "denominational colleges." Meanwhile these institutions themselves were finding that as they steadily sought to improve their academic programs, many of the best potential faculty members were persons of other religions or of no religion at all. Increasingly the Church-related colleges were confronted with a choice between being either narrowly restrictive, or of becoming general colleges for the population at large. More and more it became the case that only among the large Roman Catholic population concentrations in the East, and in the ethnic population groups in the Mid-West (especially among peoples of Scandinavian or German background) did the Church-related colleges experience in the natural course of events a continuing predominance within their faculty and student bodies of adherents to their sponsoring religious groups.

Elsewhere, especially after World War II, the expectation or requirement on the part of the Church-related colleges that their students or faculty share the beliefs or practices which had long been part of the institutions' life began to be bitterly resisted as an infringement upon personal or civil liberties. For example, in 1964, students and faculty at St. John's University in Brooklyn resisted use of Roman Catholic canon law in determining the right of students to continue in that institution. News photos appeared in papers across the country of Wake Forest students protesting the role of the Baptist Church in that college. Use of State of Maryland funds for creation of added academic facilities in several Church-related colleges of varying denominations was vigorously challenged in the courts, even after it had been shown that the institutions in question were serving a great preponderance of students of other than the colleges' own religious backgrounds, and that none of the proposed monies was to be used to create facilities either for the practice of religion or instruction in it.

A Choice for Church-related Colleges

It would appear that Church-related colleges face this choice:

(1) They may formally categorize themselves as instruments of a specific religious body. (In New York, for example, a state law provides for a religious declaration, under which a college may certify that it is controlled by and accountable to a specifically designated religious authority. It then has the right, under the law, to use religious allegiance as an admissions criterion, and to include religious beliefs and practices in its over-all required program. So far, very few institutions, either Protestant or Catholic related, have elected to make such a declaration.)

(2) Or a Church-related college or university finds that it must more and more de-emphasize the role of its sponsoring body in the areas of policy and regulation, and increasingly confine such influence to the areas of history, tradition, or atmosphere—for example, what Trinity College of Hartford calls "ties of tradition, not of law or government." [12] (These can be very powerful and effective influences, as witness the colleges of *Society of Friends* background.)

The problem in such a college then becomes (without the use of any devices which might be considered "discriminatory") to maintain a sufficiently strong and continuing "core group" so that such a body, without seeking to dominate the situation, can at least make an effective and worth-while contribution to the common life. Such a contribution, in the years now before us, will not be made by statutes or regulations imposed by institutional authority (the time for these, if it ever was, is now past). The contribution must be in the form of belief and practice, quality of life and personal witness, on the part of "a core of persons" who know God and are not ashamed to speak of Him and for Him, nor afraid to show Him forth in their own lives.

To contribute its faith to the world through such means may mean for many a Church-related institution the learning of new ways. But this is no new role for the Church. Compulsion has never been the Church's best strategy. A faith freely offered has usually been more effective than discipline or regulation, and in the end has invariably proved a more valuable contribution to the world. (It is strange that this lesson, learned in other aspects of the Church's life, should be so tardily applied to its educational institutions!)

As we look now at the second question, that of the present-day role of the Church-related college, it is plain that the functions for which most Church-related colleges were originally brought into being belonged to specific historical times and to specific geographical places. In the main these purposes have now been accomplished and of themselves no longer provide these colleges with roles as distinctive, as pressing, or as valid as formally. These "accomplished" or "outmoded" roles may be listed thus:

- (a) to provide education for a frontier, regional, or ethnic constituency for whom other educational opportunities were not available;
- (b) to educate the children of the faithful, apart from the threats to faith which were felt to be present in other college education of the time;
- (c) to evangelize for the faith;
- (d) to train future clergy.

A Two-fold New Role

But in our new materialistic and "brain-dominated" culture, a two-fold new role for the Church-related college is definitely beginning to emerge:

1. *In relation to the Church.* These colleges can now be of even greater help to the Church than the Church to them. The resources which the colleges have to offer to their churches consists of an understanding of the nature, needs, and intellectual directions of the modern world. The colleges' potential of helpfulness to the religious community consists of this point of access to, and dialogue with, the modern world. Increasingly the more sophisticated academic disciplines are forming the basis for present-day Church programs. Consider, for example, what sociology is contributing to slum and urban work, anthropology to integration and racial programs, and psychology to the Church's understanding of group dynamics. The campus-centered *avant-garde* in the arts is a chief energizer of current new trends in liturgy, music, religious drama, architecture, and symbolism. In short, a surprising number of today's most significant Church programs are at least in part "college-based."

2. *In relation to society at large.* The role of the Church-related college is no longer to carry on something equivalent to college education with all nongodly voices and challenges carefully excluded, but rather to assemble the strongest possible exposition of the full range of modern learning of all sorts, and to maintain amidst these convictions and life-styles a strong core of religious life and scholarship. Thus a Church-related college will not be a place where religious concerns are cultivated and all other views and goals subordinated or excluded altogether, but rather a place where the learning of the Church speaks to other learning and is spoken to;

where occasionally even "the religious argument" may be "slapped down"; where all cases are stated, including God's case; where the student is part of this dialogue, and whether he ends up committed or uncommitted, still learns from it intellectually and profits from it spiritually.

The Church has unique resources to contribute to this task. The trend in publicly supported education is toward steadily larger institutions and more depersonalized instruction. Church-related colleges, on the other hand, are *small* colleges. Further, religious tradition has long stressed the individual, his dignity and his importance. The Church is particularly skilled in the exercise of understanding, compassion, tolerance—care and concern for each person, one at a time. In higher education, these insights can be a great "plus" in the times into which we are moving. And most important of all, it is today becoming increasingly apparent that intellectual prowess without accompanying moral conviction offers little hope of ultimate human betterment. Church-related colleges have it within their power to bring together the highest academic excellence and their own special sense of moral commitment, and so to contribute a needed strength and quality to American education.

Future Prospects

Finally, let us consider briefly the future prospects of the Episcopal Church-related colleges in particular.

These institutions appear better adapted for significant roles in our present society than do the colleges related to many other groups.

The Episcopal Church has not in general tied its colleges tightly into the denominational structure. They have been so ordered as to appeal to a wide variety of students. They have been rather exemplary in letting objective academic qualification determine student admission and faculty appointment. As a result, increasing numbers of outstanding students who are not Episcopalians have sought to come to these colleges, and have been admitted to them.

These colleges have rather generally developed strong academic programs and some have become places of notable intellectual distinction. Three publish literary reviews which are nationally known. Two are sufficiently innovative to be grouped generally among the "experimental colleges." On all eight campuses, more valid motivations have replaced superficial high-pressure evangelism and the smug moralizing of past decades. These colleges tend to enjoy substantially greater respect in the wider academic community than do many institutions usually classified as "denominational colleges."

Today, close ecclesiastical control of academic life is neither effective nor acceptable. Enforced conformity and visibly flaunted piety are no longer impressive. Among Protestant-connected institutions, the Episcopal Church-related colleges, in company with those of the Friends, seem to be in a favorable position by virtue of their considerable experience in resting the religious case upon unostentatious, sincere, personal example, upon freedom of choice, and upon both the visible and the intangible manifestations of "the beauty of holiness."

8

CHRISTIAN WITNESS IN HIGHER EDUCATION

BY *Myron B. Bloy, Jr.*

I F ONE HAD some clear, normative definition of "Christian witness," it would then be possible to use it as a perspective from which to describe and respond to the fundamental disarray, the uncertainty about both ends and means, which characterizes contemporary higher education. On the other hand, if one had a clear, normative definition of "higher education," it would then be possible to use it as a perspective from which to describe the role which Christianity, now experiencing a breakdown of its traditional modes of self-definition, could usefully play in the academic community. But because both of the major terms of "Christian Witness in Higher Education" are deeply problematical, both moving through fundamental changes to new forms that are not at all clear now, we must be content with an extremely cautious and tentative description of their actual and possible relationships. Christianity and higher education must both learn modestly to limit their pantheons of eternal verities. Both must learn to sit loose in the intellectual saddle. This is no mere *caveat*, for if we let our natural desire for clean-cut definitions and stratagems belie the truly revolutionary changes both higher education and Christian witness are going through, we will foreclose the future, we will dampen that openness and expectancy which are necessary to the perception of new, emerging realities.

This essay will attack the problem in three steps: First, a definition of what looks like the most formative issue in higher education; second, a short analysis of the history and current state of Christian thinking about higher education; third, some concrete proposals for a functional "fit" between higher education and Christian witness.

Responsibility to Society

The elusiveness of the shape, quality, direction, and norms of American higher education is notorious. No intellectually responsible person today could adopt the serene assurance of a Cardinal Newman or a Matthew Arnold in describing the essence of higher education, either as it is or ought to be. Clark Kerr, for example, uses the cautious imprecision "multiversity" to describe what is growing to be the dominant form of American higher education, but even his own prophetic ability to see the shape of this development did not forewarn him of the revolutionary events, born mainly of problems he himself had described, on one of his own campuses. David Riesman underlines one aspect of the difficulty of comprehending American higher education by describing it as a "snake-like procession": the head is comprised of *avant-garde* institutions which are embarking on new, experimental directions, while the middle is made up of those institutions which are simply being dragged along without contributing much to the whole enterprise at all. Even this image seems a little more coherent than the real state of affairs. Many of those institutions which believe themselves to be at the head of this serpentine procession have undergone agonizing "self-study" programs which emerge with "radical" revisions in recommended goals and methods of education. But the university's astounding and continuing growth in numbers of students, in physical plant, in financial size, and in bureaucratic complexity often renders recommendations born of such self-study programs obsolete before they are instituted. These and many other factors conspire to make the image of higher education elusive in our time; it is difficult to see, in this shifting picture, where the real issues lie.

But I would suggest that the issue which, in one form or another, is increasingly at the center of this unrest in higher education is that of the responsibility of higher education—students, faculty, administrators, and institutions as a whole—to the rest of society. Up until World War II the incongruence between the university and the "real" world was tolerated with mild good humor by society. The "absent-minded professor," accepted as a social luxury in something of the same spirit as the cocker spaniel is, was long the folk symbol of this incongruence, and higher education was thought of in the public mind as a sort of finishing school for the idle rich, certainly a dispensable occupation for really serious-minded adolescents. The folk heroes of this pre-World War II culture were the rough and ready cowboy and the self-made captain of industry; both achieved their success in the world by superior moral virtue, by grit and gumption, and by native canniness. The "tin-horn" and "book-worm" were looked after with kindness (albeit, sometimes with a touch of asperity), but had no place in the dynamic affairs of real men.

World War II, and especially the Manhattan Project, changed all that, and it did so in two ways. In the first place, it became horrendously clear that the otherworldly preoccupation with esoteric games of the academic scientist and technologist could emerge in powerful and practical military form. The Dr. Frankenstein image began to compete with that of the absent-minded professor much more successfully than it had before. But in the intervening years since the Manhattan Project the person who, like the scientist and technologist, wields power successfully not only by virtue, guts, and canniness alone but by *trained intelligence* as well, has become our dominant folk image of the successful man. Fish-bowl space helmets rather than guns and holsters, and junior chemistry sets rather than puzzles, are the toys of the young. The computer programmer, the scientific and technological researcher, the city-planner, the industrial consultant, all roles demanding intelligence, trained in institutions of higher education, are the status jobs of our time. But secondly, and more important, function precedes status in this case; that is, we are fast emerging into a post-industrial, technological age where planned innovation born of trained intelligence is the key to economic and political success. Careful management, the slow accumulation of capital, luck and shrewd hunches are not enough for successful competition in this new world. Trained intelligence, able to plan and utilize innovation, is absolutely crucial to the competitive position of individuals, corporations, and nations in our time.

Thus, society will no longer allow the university to wallow in its innocuous, Mr. Chips, ivy-covered isolation because the university has become the key to society's most important status and functional needs. While the cold war was at its peak, government and foundation funds were poured into the university, and very few questions were raised, either within or outside the university, about the implications for the university of this changing role: the nation was grateful for whatever return it got on its investment and the institutions of higher education had little impetus to question their time-honored structures, goals, or styles of academic life. But now that the cold war pressure is slightly off, serious questions are being raised about the responsible use of this new power which academia has been given by society. The sharp incongruence between some of the goals of the university and society have been forced into visibility as never before. Consider, for example, the following analysis of the problem as it is seen by Alvin M. Weinberg, director of the Oak Ridge National Laboratory:

> Our society is "mission-oriented." Its mission is resolution of problems arising from social, technical, and psychological conflicts and pressures. Since these problems are not generated within any single intellectual discipline, their resolution is not to be found within a single discipline. Society's standards of achievement are set pragmatically: what works is excellent, whether or not it falls into a neatly classified discipline. In society the nonspecialist and synthesizer is king.

> The university by contrast is "discipline-oriented." Its viewpoint is the sum of the viewpoints of the separate, traditional disciplines that constitute it. The problems it deals with are, by and large, problems generated and solved within the disciplines themselves. Its standards of excellence are set by and within the disciplines. What deepens our understanding of a discipline is excellent. In the university the specialist and analyst is king.

> The structure of the discipline-oriented university and the structure of the mission-oriented society tend to be incongruent. Moreover, as the disciplines making up the university become more complex and elaborate in response to their own internal logic, the discrepancy between the university and society grows. The university becomes more remote; its connection with society weakens; ultimately it could become irrelevant. The growth of this discrepancy appears to me to be a central problem in the relation between the university

and society. It poses major difficulties for the university professor, especially in the natural sciences, who views his responsibility as a citizen broadly.[1]

Although I would question Dr. Weinberg's historical perspective (the traditional discipline-orientation of the university is lessening, but it is not doing so nearly as swiftly as our awareness of the urgency of the problem is growing), there is no doubt that he has neatly described the broad terms of the dilemma. How can the university modify its traditional focus on academic disciplines in order to participate more responsibly in the pressing "missions" of society? Further, how can it do this and maintain that "disinterested" judgment of truth which is, after all, the best gift it has to offer society?

But these questions are not being raised only by those outside the academic swim. At Massachusetts Institute of Technology, for example, these questions have been raised with accelerating urgency since World War II. There, interdisciplinary research and teaching are recognized as the most exciting areas to be in and almost all new structures for research are designated for interdisciplinary purposes. Gordon Brown, dean of the School of Engineering, is urging a reformation of the traditional discipline-orientation of the departments of engineering into such mission-oriented departments as "environmental engineering" or "energy engineering." In a speech to the American Philosophical Society, President Stratton of M.I.T. indicates some of the responsibilities, opportunities, and complex problems that await the university, particularly "the university polarized around science," as it moves into its new role. After describing several of the major problems of contemporary society such as transportation, automation, public health, urban growth, and conservation, he says:

These examples, although taken at random, exhibit certain common features. None of them falls within the domain of a traditional discipline—neither physics nor biology nor chemical engineering alone contains them. All of them touch upon areas of economics, political science, law, and management. Some involve psychology and city planning. They must be attacked from several points of view simultaneously; and these many-pronged attacks must be wisely and effectively coordinated. . . . Today only our large universities possess the necessary diversity of intellectual resources. In addition, they have accumulated in recent years invaluable experience in collaborative attacks upon the frontiers of progress. . . .

University centers for regional studies or for the economic development of new countries may be very scholarly in their character, but if their work is to be fruitful, it must link closely to the field of action. The ground, of course, is treacherous. Although a center for urban studies must not allow itself to become entangled in the politics of a particular city, the principles of urban planning cannot be developed in a scholarly vacuum. It is difficult to deal with the problems of the real world and remain aloof and untouched by that world. And so I think it inevitable that if universities engage in such undertakings, they must anticipate that step by step they will be drawn increasingly into a more direct participation in the active affairs of society.[2]

Robert C. Wood, chairman of the Department of Political Science at M.I.T., comes to the same conclusion but in more explicitly moral terms:

First, the battle ground of the United States today—the place where we will shape the quality and character of our new society—is inevitably the urban area. Second, the citadel of reason and good will within that arena is and must be the university.

In a Persuasive Society [*i.e.*, one in which decisions are made through informal colloquy because the traditional structures for decision-making no longer fit the new problems, such as those involving metropolitan areas], the critical question is always whether or not information will be available, choices determined, and attitudes shaped on the basis of wide access to facts, reasonable analysis, and reasoned debate. So, in great measure, the process of resolving our burning issues of civil rights, the ordering of urban space, the control of violence, and the building of new communities, will turn on the vigor and excellence of university participation. . . .

In these circumstances a university that does not serve its community is not a university. The advocates of the reasonable and the rational have a special duty to speak out.[3]

This awakening to the responsibilities of academia for the society, however, is not limited to administrators and faculty but extends to students as well. In fact, I would argue that it is often the students, through their civil rights and political activities (not student government politics, but *real* politics), who have prodded their adult mentors to greater concern with the problem of academic responsibility for society. Kenneth Keniston has argued that our society has produced a "youth culture," marked by lack of commitment to adult values, lack of rebelliousness, lack of admired paternal figures, social powerlessness, privatism, foreshortening of time span, and an emphasis on immediate experience which has severely limited the participation of American youth in real social issues. Erik Erikson has called this period of life in American culture a "psycho-social moratorium." University administrations, by and large, happily sanction the youth culture since it tacitly supports their *in loco parentis* power and more or less confines the problem area they have to take responsibility for to the campus and to issues of private morality.

The Free Speech Movement at the University of California in Berkeley is symbolic of a growing rebellion against the youth culture which is coming from the youth themselves. All kinds of pejorative motives have been attributed to the students involved in that rebellion, but the official report financed by a $75,000 appropriation of the Board of Regents says: "We conclude that the basic cause of unrest on the Berkeley campus was the dissatisfaction of a large number of students with many features of the society they were about to enter. This dissatisfaction led them to political action, particularly civil rights action." [4] The report also said that "We found no evidence that the Free Speech Movement was organized by the Communist Party, the Progressive Labor Movement or any other outside group." Furthermore, not only are the protest leaders at Berkeley and other campuses morally sensitive, they are also the most academically able students of all. In summarizing a five-year study of five thousand students from all over the country made by the Center for the Study of Higher Education at the University of California, *The New York Times* said, "Student leaders of campus movements demanding free speech and protesting public policies are the cream of the academic crop . . ." The *Times* report continues:

> In an interview, Dr. [Ralph] Heist [a research psychologist who led the team of investigators] said that suggestions that the Berkeley protests of last winter were staged by outside agitators "probably arose because people couldn't credit students with the ability to organize such a well-directed and meaningful and successful protest. Our study shows that they were very capable indeed," he said.

"Far from being rabble-rousers, beatniks or outside agita-
tors," Dr. Heist said, "student movement leaders tend to be
in unusually serious pursuit of education." [5]

Although some of these distinguished educators and
certainly the student protest leaders would find it strange
indeed to be described as part of the same evolutionary
development of higher education, I think there is no doubt
that both are attempting to press the university to a more
responsible, "mission-oriented" role in society. They work
at the problem in vastly different styles (a formal gathering
of the American Philosophical Society to hear a distinguished
university president lecture and a SNCC meeting to plan
a protest march are ostensibly quite different), but they are
both working from the same moral presuppositions and both
include the more able, sensitive, and dynamic members of
their respective role-groups in the academic community.

However, the future is not yet won, by a long shot: the
academic philistines, the inertia of tradition, and the contemporary difficulty in finding a judgment-empowering perspective from which to reflect sensitively on itself all inhibit
the university's effort at self-reformation. Every potential
revolutionary recognizes the philistine and the weight of
the dead hand of tradition as the enemy, but the growing
difficulty in becoming committed to any viewpoint in our
culture is a more subtle problem. Daniel Bell describes this
cultural phenomenon well when he says:

The underlying social reality, the stylistic unity of the culture of the past hundred years lies, I would argue . . . in
a structural form of expression that I have called "the eclipse
of distance," of psychic, social and esthetic distance. Modern
culture began as an effort to annihilate the contemplative

mode of experience by emphasizing *immediacy, impact, simultaneity,* and *sensation.* It is today at the point of breaking up all fixed points of reference in formal genres.[6]

Furthermore, this "eclipse of distance" is reinforced in the academic world by the paralyzing myth that commitment to "Truth" can only be undertaken by rigorously repressing commitment to any particular viewpoint on reality. Thus, scholarly "disinterestedness" and "honesty" become the grounds for disengagement from any situation demanding value judgments, and the idea of academic responsibility is reduced to such parochial matters as plagiarism and grading systems. This narrow rationalistic penchant, which disavows the larger versions of truth which can only be known through risky commitments, subtly but powerfully inhibits the university's growth towards social responsibility. I do not believe that Dr. Weinberg is correct in suggesting that the university is in danger of becoming irrelevant, but if it doesn't solve this problem of commitment it could certainly settle for an honorific but strictly passive relevance rather than a dynamic participation in society's task of determining and resolving its most pressing problems.

Whither?

In the early history of the university, the Christian perspective had an explicit and major role in molding the life of the institution. Major policy decisions were spun out of the current theological ferment. And since Christian revelation was (at least) the capstone of Truth, the best students were drawn to the study of theology. Since that time, of course, several intellectual revolutions have taken place. The Christian perspective has been typically represented by a few students, fewer faculty, and a chaplain, who have gathered in denominationally segregated, self-protective enclaves on the edges of campuses. The main function of these enclaves was to provide "fellowship" for those denominational students who couldn't get it elsewhere and a place for pastoral counselling about personal problems for those students who didn't otherwise have access to a sensitive adult. These enclaves were certainly not at the intellectual center of the life of the university, but there is no doubt that in the period before the university itself became seriously concerned about the social and psychological life of the students they had a crucial function. Now, however, the universities are falling all over themselves in catering to the student's "extra-curricular" life: plush student unions, replete with bowling alleys, cozy lounges, and professional organizers of student activities, stand in raw grandeur on campuses everywhere; new dormitory buildings are designed with one eye cocked on the principles of group dynamics; and psychiatric services, just recently totally absent from the campus, are doing a booming business in every major university. At M.I.T., for example, the psychiatry department is concerned not only about the truly psychotic student, but also about those who encounter relatively minor psychological problems in the course of their academic career; as a result, one out of every seven M.I.T. students visits an Institute psychiatrist at least once while they are at M.I.T. Furthermore, there is less and less social stigma associated with psychiatric treatment; indeed, sometimes it seems that it is a mark of prestige. Naturally, this development has seriously challenged the fellowship/personal counselling role of the traditional chaplain-led student religious enclave. "Canterbury Clubs" are declining and dying everywhere.

The intellectual role of Christianity has also undergone some radical changes. A few years ago it was still believed by many university Christians (students, faculty, and chaplains) that the traditional apologetic rendering of Christianity fulfilled its intellectual function on the campus. It was thought, in other words, that a "relevant," felicitous interpretation of the major Christian doctrines in the light of the university's life was the key intellectual strategy of Christianity on the campus. One of the best documents to emerge from that strategy was *The Faith, the Church and the University: A Report of a Conversation Among University Christians;*[7] it was the result of two colloquies involving distinguished Episcopalian leaders in the Christian concern for higher education. Jones Shannon, executive director of the Church Society for College Work and a participant in those colloquies, says now about the Report:

> Considerable anxiety was expressed symptomatically about the university in the Report, but the prescriptive suggestions seem, in retrospect, insufficient, while the report's theological reflection seems calm and serene. If the report were undertaken today, I suspect the results would be reversed in the direction of less tendency to prescribe how American education should administer itself, and toward more attention to the chaos and conflict in present theological reflection.[8]

It is clearly no longer possible to dwell, in intellectual comfort and serenity, in a Christian doctrinal bastion from which we can dispense *noblesse oblige* advice to the university.

Now, what do we make of this institutional and intellectual disarray of the Christian perspective in the contemporary university? In the first place, we should be thankful that the university has accepted a social and psychological concern for students as part of its legitimate business. To a certain extent, the Church has been a pace-setter for the university here: for example, the "Technology Christian Association" was the center of student extra-curricular life at M.I.T. long before the Institute took any serious official responsibility for that side of student life. Furthermore, we should be happy to move out of a fellowship-creating role. Valid as it is in many respects, it has tended to be a strong conservative support of the "youth culture" which the best students are increasingly abjuring. Chaplains should also be happy to take less responsibility for counselling students about their personal problems, partly because psychiatrists are much better at it than chaplains and partly because it is essentially a passive symptom-focused function which has often inhibited chaplains from becoming involved in the intellectual and policy issues of university life. In fact, to be seriously concerned about the psychic health of students is to be involved precisely with those intellectual and policy issues which affect the total character of a given university's life, rather than only to respond to those individuals who have developed personal problems as a result of the inadequacies of university life. The development of this social and psychiatric concern on the part of the university must be seen for what it really is, namely, the grace of God at work in behalf of man.

In the second place, the intellectual disarray of Christianity in our time may be God's cleansing fire that is clearing the way for the recovery of a dynamic Christian witness rather than an unmitigated disaster for the Church. The typical apologetic gambits of the Church have for years been becoming less and less persuasive to the non-believers in the university, but now, at long last, they aren't even persuasive for us Christians. We can now begin to build our ministry, our witness, out of the few bed-rock assertions that we can honestly make rather than try to defend the whole cumbersome intellectual establishment that we have inherited. William Hamilton has described this historical situation as one in which we can come to grasp the essence of Christianity for our day only by "being willing to admit that our knowledge and our faith are in bits and pieces; being content with this weakness; clarifying the little we can know; speaking about it as openly as we can; listening to the other as often as we speak." [9] This can be a frightening or an exhilarating time for Christians in the university, and I expect that it is a little of both for most of us. We are, to use a bizarre but (for me) effective image, intellectually skinny-dipping: although one is somewhat chary of being caught by inquisitive eyes while swimming naked in a not quite remote pool, the sense of strength and freedom in swimming without that soggy, wool symbol of propriety is gloriously exhilarating. The psychological trick is to minimize the fear and maximize the exhilaration. Christians today are intellectually skinny-dipping perforce in the academic pool, and it is exhilarating for those who accept this situation as a gift from God.

The very best theological statement of what Christian witness *can* be in the university and of what, in fact, it is actually *becoming* in many places is the so-called "Presence Document" which was painfully hammered out at the 1964 General Committee meeting of the World Student Christian Federation in Embalse Rio Tercero, Argentina. In comparison with the usual fustian style and sweeping assertions of official Christian documents, the simplicity and humility of this statement is miraculous; it represents the approach that Professor Hamilton describes above. As much recent theology does, it also finds its authority more squarely on the contagious quality of Jesus' "presence" as an empowering norm for human maturity than on appeals to metaphysical proofs. Here are some key sections from that document:

The Federation in its aims and practice has always been concerned with making Jesus Christ known in the academic world. "Evangelization," "witness," and "mission" have long been among the words used to describe this task. But these words have now become problematic for many students. This dissatisfaction springs from the historical burden which they carry and which suggests a Christian behaviour of speaking before listening, of calling people away from their natural communities into a Christian grouping, and of a preoccupation with the soul at the expense of the whole of life. Even when the words "witness" and "mission" are properly understood, many students feel that they are too big and too definite. They suggest a certainty of faith and purpose, and an ability to conceptualize faith in terms which create difficulty for many people, not least for those most committed to Christ and his gospel.

When we try to find words in the living language of today to describe the task of the Christian community in the academic world, we seek to give expression to the same realities as our forefathers knew, *i.e.*, to witness to our belief that in Christ Jesus God has reconciled the world to himself. In this document, we use the word "presence" for that reality. We use it to express both the centre of Christian faith and our response to it. As an expression of our faith, it points to the incarnation: God became man like us and lived among us. The man Jesus uncovers life for us . . . His presence has shown God to us.

And even after his death he is present, we are told, and goes his quiet way through history. His community has always perceived signs of his presence, but it has had no proofs. . . . His friends in the world, be they a parish church or a student group, have accepted and recognized their God in the man Jesus, and have set out to follow him.

We use the word "presence" to describe that way of life. It does not mean that we are simply there; it tries to describe the adventure of being there in the name of Christ, often anonymously, listening before we speak, hoping that men will recognize Jesus for what he is and stay where they are, involved in the fierce fight against all that dehumanizes, ready to act against demonic powers, to identify with the outcast, merciless in ridiculing modern idols and new myths. When we say "presence," we say that we have to get into the midst of things even when they frighten us. Once we are there, we may witness fearlessly to Christ if the occasion is given; we may also be silent. "Presence" for us means "engagement," involvement in the concrete structures of our society. It indicates a priority. First, we have to be there before we can see our task clearly. In one sense of the word, presence precedes witness. In another sense, the very presence is witness. For us, to be present in the name of Christ spells death to the *status quo*, both in society and in the Christian community; we will not tire of pleading and working for the restoration of normal manhood as we see it in Jesus. But our presence is grounded in no comfortable optimism. From what happened to the Lord, we know what resistance and opposition to expect. And as for our weak faith, our poverty of understanding of what we believe, we trust that while present we will be given new words or an authentic silence.[10]

A Functional "Fit"

Finally, I would suggest that there is a functional "fit" between, on the one hand, the contemporary university, struggling for a socially responsible role against its own philistines, its congealed traditions, and the cultural and academic forces which inhibit its commitment to judgment-empowering perspectives, and, on the other hand, contemporary Christianity, now stripped of much of its protective doctrine and rediscovering its life in commitment to Jesus as the empowering norm, the "presence," for human maturity. This Christian perspective, freed of much cumbersome intellectual posturing, is, in fact, a clear (but not rigid), flexible (but not indefinable), and dynamic (but not fa-

natic) option for commitment which can be extremely helpful for the university in its struggle for social responsibility.
It can be helpful through the actions Christians take in
behalf of specific, concrete issues in the university's evolutionary growth towards its new role, but I think its weight
can be felt even more as university Christians implicitly
witness to the *possibility* for others of holding a judgment-
empowering commitment, *i.e.,* a commitment serving an
intellectually valid function in the life of the university.
This is the version of being "fools for Christ's sake" which
is appropriate for the academic world, and perhaps Christians who are willing to take this risk (a risk of much greater
proportions than those outside the academic swim realize)
will serve as encouragement to others in the university to
uncover and clarify their own inarticulate commitments and
to test them as perspectives for helping the university to
achieve a more significant role in our culture.

Clearly the "fit" I describe demands a much more mature,
intellectually able, and culturally perceptive Christian witness than is now evident on most campuses, but the relationship between the university's need and the theological
development I have described is gradually becoming clearer,
and there are signs on campuses here and there that these
two are meeting. One or two examples will indicate how this
is happening. One of the problems for the students who are
strong enough to revolt against the youth culture in behalf
of a more serious participation in society is that they find
very few adult mentors who share their passion and anger
but who are also able to act out of a mature, emotionally
steady, judgment-empowering perspective. Some Christian
faculty members and chaplains on a number of campuses are
providing just this kind of help for these students. For
example, I know one large metropolitan university where
two chaplains are just about the only adults in the institution

who are really respected by the student leaders of the civil rights and freedom movements. They are respected because they share the prophetic vision of the students and are not afraid to act out of it. Their main function is to provide a coherent and consistent, yet broad and flexible, perspective on the inchoate character of the struggle the students find themselves in. They are deeply involved in a counselling role, but it is not nearly so overtly religious or so individualistic as it once was: instead of the relaxed discussion in the pastor's hushed study with an individual about his personal problems, these chaplains are much more likely to find themselves involved in a heated debate (at 3 A.M. around a mimeographing machine) with a group of student civil rights leaders about the strategic implications of the wording of a flier urging students to participate in the picketing of a local school committee which tolerates racially imbalanced schools. (This, incidentally, is an example of how chaplains, who have tended to bemoan their anomalous, status-less role in the university, can put that role to effective use. Chaplains, by and large, have much more freedom than they usually dare to use.) Unfortunately, not many Christian students have found their way into such activities, but a few have and hopefully more will follow as the "image" of Christianity becomes more dynamic.

At M.I.T. several of the faculty and I have formed an interdisciplinary, faculty Seminar on Technology and Culture which meets monthly to hear a talk and to discuss some aspect of the impact of technology on our culture. The seminar involves about forty faculty members from almost every department. After more than a year of this cumulative effort we are all more sensitive to the kind of influence M.I.T. does, can, and ought to have on our culture. Although religious persuasion is not a criterion for membership in the seminar, and although the relation of technology to religion is only one of many aspects of the problem that we discuss, the seminar was originally conceived out of the Christian perspective and that perspective is represented well by several members of the seminar. Just as the Christian perspective functions to support the undergraduate protest leaders in their effort to bring students generally into deeper participation in society's problems, so it can function to help faculty to enlarge their competence and concern in "mission-oriented" areas.

Certainly these and similar developments do not add up to a revolution in Christian witness in higher education, but I believe they point to the most relevant kind of role that the Christian perspective can fill in the life of the university today, a role which can be exhilarating indeed for those Christians with an inclination to skinny-dipping.

9

THE CHURCH AND THEOLOGICAL EDUCATION

BY *Wood B. Carper, Jr.*

FOR THE purpose of this essay, "theological education" means simply that effort on the part of the seminaries of the Episcopal Church to prepare men for Holy Orders: that is to say, to give them the knowledge and the appropriate skills for an adequate performance of the duties of a Deacon, Priest, or Bishop in the Church of God as that Church is understood by those who stand within the Anglican Communion, and who continue to cherish its faith and order. In these days of theological "ferment" and rapid social change it may be difficult to ascertain who those are, but there has been as yet no mass exodus from the doctrine, discipline, and worship explicit or implicit in the Book of Common Prayer. Presumably the Church still wants men who can answer affirmatively the solemn questions asked by an ordaining bishop[1] and meet the "Normal Standard of Learning" specifically stated in Canon 29.[2] A seminary true to its calling will take seriously the warning

> Take heed that the persons, whom ye present unto us, be apt and meet, for their learning and godly conversa-

138

tion, to exercise their Ministry duly, to the honour of
God, and the edifying of his Church.[3]

The need for special institutions for the training of the
clergy was recognized by the Roman Church as early as 1563
when the Council of Trent promulgated a canon directing
bishops to set up schools designed to overcome the appalling unfitness, intellectual and moral, of the sixteenth-century
ecclesiastics. The very word "seminary" comes from a phrase
in this canon, that the school should be "a perpetual seed-
plot of ministers of God," *Dei ministrorum perpetuum
seminarium.*[4] Quite naturally these schools were patterned
along monastic lines, with monastic ideals of perfection
their goal, personal holiness directed toward a pastoral ministry in a parochial setting. St. Mary's Seminary in Baltimore,
Maryland, founded in 1791, was the first of the many Roman
Catholic "houses of priestly formation" now established in
the United States.[5]

It was not until the early part of the nineteenth century
that the non-Roman Churches considered seminaries essential for the education of the clergy. As long as the colleges
and universities maintained a churchly character and connection it was possible for men to obtain theological education as part of their liberal arts courses, then acquire
sufficient clerical skills from association with practicing
clergymen and their own experience. When, for one reason
or another, the colleges and universities no longer taught
theology and generally severed their Church relationship—
the state universities, of course, had none—the founding of
denominational seminaries began. One of the earliest was
Andover (Congregational), founded in 1808. The Episcopal
Church, slowly recovering from the birth-pangs of independence from the Church of England, authorized the
founding of its first seminary in the General Convention of

1817. By 1819 the General Theological Seminary was in operation, and in 1823 another, The Protestant Episcopal Seminary in Virginia, was established. It could be said that the Episcopal Church has been more successful in authorizing and founding seminaries than it has been in maintaining and nourishing them, though at the present time the eleven accredited schools seem to be in fair enough health. Though none of them receives direct support from the National Church except—and that just recently—in the form of scholarship aid, they have been able to survive on the legacies and gifts of concerned members of the Church.[6]

Since no one person can speak authoritatively for all these schools, even for one of them, let me immediately exonerate all my colleagues who are currently teaching in them from any responsibility for the opinions and judgments which follow. I hope that many will agree with me, but I know from personal experience that "American faculty members do not readily come to a common outlook or agreement." [7] I suspect, however, that there is wider agreement on the aims of seminary education in the Episcopal Church today than there has been in the not-too-distant past. I believe that there is less party-spirit, and considerably more mutual trust today than there was thirty years ago when I was a seminarian. If this is not wishful thinking, perhaps our notions about the end-product of our educational efforts, the man who will be ordained, will be in general agreement.

The Ideal Training for Ministry

It seems to me, then, that a great deal of the masochistic self-criticism which characterizes much of the current studies of seminary education[8] could be turned to more constructive channels by taking a calmer, though not complacent, view of the situation. A time of crisis is no time for panic, and Christians, of all people, should be immune to failure of nerve. A help toward achieving confidence and courage is the assumption I make that not everything in Christian thought and history is a mistake, and least of all a mistake in the traditional ideal for the ordained minister. In words used by John Henry Hobart at the formal opening of General Seminary, he should be learned, orthodox, pious, and practical, and a seminary should be a place where he can be helped to become just that.

Hobart, of course, did not invent the ideal. In a broad sense, however, the qualities described have been those pleaded for in all the treatises on the clergy since the Epistles to Timothy. Indeed, for back in time before the Christian era the human need for an institution composed of a corps of men and/or women set apart for leadership in dealing with relationships between men and God or gods has been seen, and the need met in the ministry of priests or priestesses. "They are set apart for the specific purpose of establishing, maintaining and restoring intercourse and adjustment between the sacred and secular spheres, theistically interpreted in terms of a personal Deity at once transcendent and immanent." [9] These words of Professor James will not impress those who have dismissed the distinction between sacred and secular, but they seem to me to express what the Church intends when one of her bishops says "Receive the Holy Ghost for the Office and Work of a Priest in the Church of God, now committed unto thee by the imposition of our hands." [10] They mean what St. Chrysostom meant when he wrote *On the Priesthood;* what St. Gregory the Great meant when he wrote *The Pastoral Rule;* what George Herbert meant when he wrote *The Country Parson;* and they mean what seems to me to be the axis around which the many activities of ministry may revolve without flying off on tangents: an Office and Work which is con-

cerned with the pastoral care of human beings in their
earthly pilgrimage.

To implement this ideal is extraordinarily difficult. Perhaps the reason for this is hinted at in St. Gregory's remark
that "the care of souls is the art of arts," and great artists
are not easily come by in any field. There is, however, good
reason to rejoice in the occasional appearance of true and
God-given greatness, and not to be down-hearted about
the multitudes who may not achieve greatness but who can
achieve competence. It has been said that everybody can
learn to draw because everybody can learn to write. This
is comforting to a teacher of other arts than drawing, and
should encourage the seminaries to believe they can produce
men who are competent if not exceptional.

Perhaps a brief exploration of the four adjectives used
by Bishop Hobart will reveal the dimension of the task laid
on seminaries, and reduce some of the utopian expectations
which are the bases of much criticism to manageable proportions. At any rate it should show that there are unavoid-
able tensions in which seminary students and faculties must
live as happily and creatively as possible.

The word "learned" for the seminaries is defined by
Canon 29 as a superstructure of specifically Christian knowledge solidly based on what used to be called a liberal education, an education which gave a man a grasp of the world
in which he lived. Normally he got that grasp in four or
more years of college work leading to a bachelor's degree.
This is generally a prerequisite for admission to seminary.
It is notorious that there is great variation in both the
content and the quality of these degrees. The desired base is
often very shaky indeed in such areas as philosophy, ancient
or modern languages, history, and even English composi-
tion and spelling. It would be possible, of course, by having
a rigid and ruthless admissions policy, to eliminate men

whose prior education would handicap them in seminary, but since there are other qualifications for an effective ministry than a broad cultural education, this solution is not likely to be attempted.

Therefore the seminaries must cope with a wide variety of educational backgrounds as they lead men for three years through the areas of study laid down by the canon. They cannot be completely "remedial," but they can help, and a system of individual tutorial instruction, such as that at General Seminary, can sometimes accomplish wonders. Men do overcome handicaps as they also attain an adequate grasp on the biblical, historical, and theological materials the seminary course requires. The thorny problem of how to integrate the relatively new areas of knowledge, psychology, and sociology, which are so important for a modern man's understanding of himself and his society, into the classical theological scheme has not been solved to anybody's satisfaction, but the search for a solution is not being neglected. For many reasons it seems unlikely that more years can be added to the seminary course: the men have already had four or more years of college, present facilities could not accommodate additional classes,[11] and various psychological factors would probably dull the edge of the mind's endeavors—few people want to be in school all their lives!

The word "orthodox" is having a rough time these days, but it is important in that it points to the fact that the seminaries are the Church's schools, and are responsible to it for producing men who are committed to the truth of the message they will swear to proclaim and the validity and efficacy of the sacraments they will administer. Here the tensions are indeed high and will probably get higher, since definitely "unorthodox" opinions are being published by highly placed persons in the Church, and are apparently being read by large numbers of people.[12] Orthodox arguments against these opinions are not lacking,[13] but probably will not be heard by so wide an audience. In the long run the debate will undoubtedly help the Church clarify its thinking, but, in the meantime, the seminarians have a grand opportunity to become even more confused than they normally are, and faculties have a grave responsibility to help them maintain some equilibrium. This is especially true in regard to their appropriation of the "new morality" without a very serious consideration of the old, and the quality of simple goodness will be sacrificed on the dubious altar of "identification with the world." [14]

Living in "out of joint times" is never a comfortable experience, and seminaries are not the ivory towers they are often claimed to be. Integrity, however, is a higher value than comfort. Thus, in my opinion, the seminaries should continue to strive to produce men, learned and orthodox, who can live under the tensions until the unforeseen resolution arrives.

The word "pious" points to the fact that theological education can never be simply a matter of the mastery of a number of subjects as mental exercises, but must also be deeply concerned with the spiritual growth of all the members of the seminary, convinced that the man of God should be a godly man. It is this which distinguishes a true seminary from a graduate school of theology, though a true seminary may also have a graduate department and devote part of its energies to the training of scholars for research and teaching. This means that the chapel and what it stands for must be as central in actuality as it usually is architecturally.

Achieving this centrality is much more difficult to accomplish than it is to realize that in some way it must be accomplished. The old ideal of an ordered devotional life in a supporting community places heavy pressures on men already pressured by academic and, increasingly, family re-sponsibilities. Most students are not monks and do not intend to become such. Yet, I am convinced that the chief reason why "ministers break down" is the fact that either they never developed or gradually lost their capacity to pray, rather than that they were overwhelmed by the demands of their jobs. If this be true, it would seem that a reduction in the number of hours required in classrooms would be a better solution than accepting defeat in the life of prayer.

In support of the goal of producing men who will con-tinually seek by prayer, more will be needed than regular chapel services and talks recommending a spiritual rule of life. The development of an ascetic theology suitable for the conditions of modern life and its inclusion in curricula even at the expense of dislocating something else is essential, and not simply as an "elective" for the specially devout. If we cannot get men who can pray and can teach others to pray, who can develop a style of life attractive because it is God-centered, no matter how competent we make them in other fields, we shall miss the heart of the matter. Our men must be priests in the right sense—men devoted and rightly set apart. We must help them to become competent not only in proclaiming the faith but in nourishing a genu-inely religious life in the faithful. It has been said that the lives of Christians will have to be the parables of the King-dom for mid-twentieth century, and perhaps the best step toward the solution of the problem of evangelism would be the revival of the old work of spiritual direction, under the modern name of "coach." [15]

Bishop Hobart's fourth adjective, "practical," indicates that the seminary graduate is supposed to be able to prac-tice, and that the seminary help him to become a practi-tioner, a professional. It is not too difficult, though it is time-consuming, to teach men how to perform their duties as leaders of the public worship of the Church and to administer sacraments. It is very difficult to teach them to preach effectively, to translate their newly acquired professional vocabulary into words people without professional training may understand. (It has always been popular to criticize preachers. St. Augustine has a scathing passage in his *Christian Doctrine*[16] which is rather unfair of him since he had been a professor of rhetoric before he became a Christian preacher!) It is not too difficult to introduce them to their duties as administrators of the parishes in which most of them will serve. It is very difficult to teach them to be good teachers of the teachers who will help them instruct young and old alike. It is exceedingly difficult to teach them to be good pastors, for, to cite St. Gregory again, this is "the art of arts." Summer programs of supervised experience in parishes, hospitals, and penal institutions are used by all the seminaries to provide an understanding of personal relations which cannot be gained in a classroom or from reading a book. Yet these programs in addition to the work outside the seminaries most of the men do, commonly called "field education," can keep them involved in the ongoing lives of people.

"Practical" does not necessarily mean that which is immediately and obviously useful, in terms of that kind of success which can be measured by bigger budgets and larger congregations. These are not to be despised, provided that all efforts to gain quality are not sacrificed to those for quantity. Unless the seminaries insist on this and resist the pressures upon them to turn out mechanics, we shall not achieve the aims of theological education. Parish administration is a legitimate field of study, provided it is not confused with business administration. Christian education is a legitimate field of study provided it is not confused with school management in the sense of the size and placing of chairs and the tint of what used to be called unambiguously a blackboard. I am confident that the Episcopal seminaries are avoiding these kinds of errors.

The purpose of an ideal is to give shape and direction to the necessarily imperfect actions of men, though not to encourage them to relax their efforts to approach the ideal simply because they have it. What I have sketched above seems to me to give direction and shape to theological education which can bring into focus the blurred image of the work of the ordained man, an image satirized by Martin Thornton as "the current idea of some chaotic admixture of preaching, teaching, evangelism, writing, study, sociology, good work, tea parties, and youth work." [17] Bishop Hobart's adjectives do not describe four divisible functions—"you be learned and I'll be pious"—but four qualities of one function, that of being a priest in the Church of God, not simply a pastoral director with some priestly duties. That is to say, a man with that hard-to-define but not-to-be-missed quality of respect for his office and respect for his people; a man who knows himself as a human being in the twentieth century, and as such knows himself called by God to be a priest in the twentieth century, normally responsible for the well-being of a "flock" solemnly committed to him.

After nearly ten years of teaching in a seminary, I am not as impatient as I once was about the present ways of training our priests, for I have come to see what I always should have seen, that each one of our choices of what to emphasize involves the sacrifice of some value. Whereas we would like to have "both/and," in practice it often comes down to an "either/or." We simply cannot do all things for all men, and the complete parson cannot be turned out in three years. He must continue to grow on his own, and he can find help and refreshment in the increasing number of educational opportunities offered by the seminaries and other institutions. If in his seminary years he can be helped to form some good habits and good attitudes, he will have got the best that men can give him. Then if he is at all open to God and to men, he will adequately serve both.

An Argument from Continuity

I suppose it is amply clear that I do not think that priesthood is outmoded and therefore irrelevant for "mankind come of age," whatever that phrase really means. I should like to make it equally clear, in concluding this essay, that I am not impressed by and certainly not intimidated by the assertions that we are training men for a nineteenth-century ministry, that the parochial system has broken down, that there are no "viable" institutions in which an ordained ministry can function. I take it that any version of Christianity is inescapably social and that therefore it must express its sociality by gathering together otherwise separated individuals for the express purpose of worship, the hearing of God's Word and making Eucharist being the usual method of worshipping. It need not be in a Gothic church or in a catacomb, but the gathering must take place, and when it does, it is the local manifestation of the Church. That is all that a parish is and all it is meant to be, the assembly of Christ's people. If it has, and accepts, geographical responsibility, so much the better. Wherever people are they are not out of geography, unless of course they are in some astronautical orbit. If the assembly has a place—it need not be elaborate—so much the better, even if the "place" is relatively mobile.

There is, it seems to me, considerably more continuity than discontinuity in human history, especially in regard to the institutions men inevitably erect. At any rate we must start from where we are, adapting our institutions as best we can to changing needs. I myself find it heartening that Abbé Michonneau named his great book *Revolution in a City Parish*,[18] not "revolt from one," and that the very word "parish" was born not in rural England, but in the teeming and complicated cities of the ancient world. The urbanization of the modern world has created fantastic problems for the people who live in the new Babylons, especially for those who have a nostalgia for an imaginary rural Eden, but since the parishes were born in cities, we can legitimately hope that they can once more learn to live in them. Certainly it would be the height of irresponsibility to shirk the effort to try.[19]

That theological education be improved is, of course, the hope of faculties and students alike. Just how to do it is the problem. Most suggestions come in the line of proposals that are impossible to effectuate without an amount of money and an increase in trained personnel that are beyond the reach of any particular institution. This is true of the educational institutions in America from grammar schools through graduate schools. All are pretty much in the same boat, and must row through the same stormy seas. But they need not founder if they keep on rowing. The popularity of the word "crisis," whether in United Nations chamber or classroom, should not weaken the Christian belief that the ultimate crisis was met and overcome when a Galilean Jew was "crucified under Pontius Pilate" for "us men and our salvation." It is in this affirmation of faith that the Church lives and her seminaries operate.

PART III
Liturgy, Society, and Mission

10
LITURGY AND THE EDUCATIONAL PROCESS

BY *H. Boone Porter, Jr.*

LITURGY and Christian education touch each other at many points. At the most mundane level, there is the vexatious problem of scheduling classes at approximately the same hour as services of worship on Sunday morning. At the most elevated level, there is the Christian certainty that all creation is called to find its fulfilment in the glorification of God, and hence that all education must ultimately be education for worship. In between the sublime and the ridiculous, there is a variety of day-to-day questions which clergy and laity must face in a constructive way.[1] The present inquiry will concern itself mainly with two aspects of the matter: the age-old question of whether liturgy should be utilized as a medium for teaching, and the new question of the effect of the changes being introduced by the contemporary Liturgical Movement. First, however, some preliminary definitions will be useful.

Christian worship is the glorification of Almighty God our heavenly Father, through the mediation of Jesus Christ our Lord and Saviour, in the fellowship of the Holy Spirit who

153

unites us to Christ and to one another. Such worship should of course characterize the whole scope of the Christian life. Its explicit formulation in words and actions is the liturgy. Because of the Christian dedication of the First Day of the biblical week—Sunday—to the service of God, and especially the morning of this day, Christian liturgy finds its standard and normative embodiment in the traditional pattern of public worship on Sunday morning. Since the earliest times, this pattern has consisted of two halves.[2] The first, or Ministry of the Word, is characterized by the reading of scripture and preaching. Psalms and hymns are also sung, and prayers are said. The second half, or Ministry of the Sacrament, involves the offering of bread and wine, their consecration in a solemn priestly prayer of thanksgiving, and the distribution of this sacred food and drink to the worshippers. Considered objectively, this sequence of words and actions, and only this sequence, can be called the historic pattern of Christian worship. This alone, furthermore, is the ecumenical pattern, for nothing else can command, as this has, the acceptance of the overwhelming majority of Christians. Any discussion of liturgy must begin with this clear understanding, and Christian teachers, as they train a future generation of responsible Christian people, cannot emphasize this too strongly.

Is Liturgy a Means of Teaching?

It would seem at first sight that the relation between this classic pattern of worship and Christian education would be very simple. The first half, or Ministry of the Word, is not purely didactic in character, but it is very largely so. It derives historically from the Jewish synagogue, which was, and still is, largely educational in purpose. In contemporary Jewish colloquial speech, synagogue is called *schule*—

"school." Here then is the specifically teaching part of the liturgy. It would seem equally clear that the second half of the rite is sacrificial in purpose. Because it is an act of consecration to God, the worshippers ought not to seek from it pragmatic benefits for themselves. The second half, in short, is directed towards the adoration of God, not the training of the worshippers.

This basic differentiation in emphasis between the two halves of the liturgy is indeed important. The widespread disregard of it in the recent past has weakened our understanding both of the liturgy and of the Christian faith itself. The Epistle and Gospel must be clearly and intelligently read to the people, and the understanding of these lections almost always requires some elucidation in the sermon.[3] Preachers must especially address themselves to the dramatic character of the Holy Gospel as an expression of the Risen Christ speaking to us in our midst.

The restoration of a due appreciation for the Ministry of the Word deserves a high priority, but this does not settle the whole question of the educational dimensions of the liturgy. What is didactic may not, in the long run, be the most educative. Having been instructed, and having been brought into God's presence, by scripture and preaching, we proceed to adore Him at the altar. In the outpouring of self in the adoration of God, we learn to know Him as He is. People in fact learn Christianity, and learn about Christianity, by the act of worshipping. The corporate repetition of liturgical words and actions week after week, and the variations introduced by the yearly cycle of special seasons and feasts, when experienced over and over during a lifetime, constitutes one of the most powerful educational systems ever devised. Yet its peculiar force lies in the fact that it is not contrived for this purpose.[4] God, not the worshipper, is the center of worship. If the attention is shifted to the worshipper, the reality of worship is soon lost, and the lesson in God's centrality is lost too.

During the course of Christian history, we see a variety of efforts to safeguard this transcendent quality of liturgical worship. In the classical Reformed Churches, children and unconverted adults were not even allowed to remain in the building while the Lord's Supper was being celebrated. Roman Catholicism, at the other extreme, has not suffered from this unfortunate aversion to children and to sinners, and all its people are encouraged to attend Mass often. Yet the latter, until the present time, has been superbly safeguarded: it has been for the most part silent, in a language understood only by the priest, and in the framework of ceremonies the meaning of which, in some cases, was known to no one. Here apparently was the ultimate divorce between liturgy and education! Yet, as everyone knows, the Latin Mass was for centuries a most powerful factor in the inculcation and formation of Roman Catholic spirituality. Its great impact on people has been in no small part the result of its disregard of the worshipper: its supernatural intention has been unequivocal. Today the Roman Mass is being reformed generally along the lines indicated by liturgical scholarship. The Ministry of the Word, the first half of the Mass, has been restored to the vernacular and is now largely directed toward the edification of the clergy[5] and people. The second half, containing the Latin Canon, retains a reserved character.

That regular liturgical worship has a powerful effect on people cannot be denied.[6] The question is, What sort of effect does a particular way of worshipping have? The Church cannot disregard its responsibility for the character and quality of this effect. An obvious example lies in the degree of decorum and dignity required of people in church. This undoubtedly imparts a special feeling, but what sort of feeling? Is the behavior of a congregation such that people love God's house as a place of order and peace, or is it such that people suppose that only the well-dressed and well-mannered are welcome at services? Often it is the latter.

Another example is equally ominous. Most Churchmen, on an average week, only see their priest on Sunday morning, when he is dressed in impressive garments and is taking the leading role in the sanctuary. This unquestionably and inevitably causes people to view him, as they should, in a special light—but what sort of light? Does his role in the sanctuary make his people feel a deep spiritual identification with the solemn words and actions which he performs in their name? Or does something in his voice and manner lead to the feeling that religious affairs are his little domain, in which the active cooperation of the laity is neither desired nor needed? It must be sadly confessed that the latter is in fact the impression often conveyed.

Precisely because attendance at church on Sunday is for most people the principal time for religious reflection and the most usual form of contact with the Church as an organized body, even small details in the service can have an unexpected importance. A misunderstanding created in a private pastoral conference may mislead one person—but in such a setting the individual can easily ask for clarification. On the other hand, a misunderstanding unconsciously built up in church on repeated Sunday mornings can mislead an entire congregation, and no one will presume to challenge it. Anyone who is concerned with Christian education must ponder this.

The Response of the Liturgical Movement

The kind of problem we have been describing calls for a two-fold solution. On the one hand, the Church, through its hierarchy and legislative synods, must see to it that its formularies and practices, in liturgy and in other matters, actually do express to people what they are intended to express. Since the meanings of words and actions are constantly subject to gradual changes, periodic liturgical revision is necessary. On the other hand, official prescriptions, no matter how well enunciated, cannot preclude misuse and misinterpretation.[7] Hence the clergy and people of every local congregation must subject themselves, their views, and their practices to critical self-examination to discover whether what goes on in their parish is in fact providing the good Christian nurture which they intend. This kind of reappraisal, at both the constitutional and the local levels, is a matter of major concern to the contemporary Liturgical Movement.

At what may be called the constitutional level, this movement urges the revision of the Book of Common Prayer and the analogous liturgical books of other Christian bodies. Since Christian worship involves the dedication of all life to God, through Christ, in the power of His Spirit, the complete renewal of liturgy ultimately involves the renewal of the entire worshipping Church and the renewal of the human society in which Christians live and work. Viewed in this light, the revision of service-books is but a small facet of the total objective and purpose of the Liturgical Movement. This fact has not hitherto been understood by many American Churchmen. These wider goals, however, must not obscure the fact that our Prayer Book will undoubtedly be revised within the next decade or so, and the changes will be rather considerable. At the same time, and for closely related reasons, Church music is changing, Church architecture is changing, and ideas about ceremonial and the furnishing of the sanctuary are changing. We live in a new age, and in many ways it is a wonderful and creative age. This affects religion, as it affects other aspects of life. All this has tremendous implications for the teacher.

It must be frankly conceded that in many parishes this constitutes a problem, for the customary practices and arrangements for worship are still those inherited from the last century. The Victorian age had many fine qualities, but unfortunately it was also distinguished by clumsiness, ostentation, and sentimentality. Such an atmosphere does not and cannot commend itself to most people today. We have tried too long to train Christians of the present century to worship like Christians of the last century. The fact is that we must now begin to train them for the twenty-first century. Many parishes are woefully unprepared for the task, yet there it is. The future faces us with the eschatological words of the familiar children's game: "Here I come—ready or not!"

How is the teacher of today to train people for the unborn liturgy of tomorrow? Actually, the problem is not so obscure. Informed liturgical scholars everywhere insist that the purpose of current liturgical revision is to provide a clear and contemporary formulation of the traditional rites. This applies especially to the principal service of Christian worship, the Holy Eucharist. As we have said earlier, there is no doubt as to the historic and ecumenical order for public worship on Sunday morning: the holy scriptures read and expounded in a context of prayer and praise, followed by the solemnity of the Breaking of Bread. The teacher who has meditated on this fundamental order, and related his or her spiritual apprehensions to it, will be well prepared for future liturgical developments. More important still, the pupils of such a teacher will also be well prepared.

So much for the question of the official revision of the liturgy. Let us now return to the obligation of the local congregation to scrutinize its arrangements for worship and to see what effect they are having on its people. In past generations, such a procedure was unthinkable in most parishes. Worship followed a fixed and unchanging pattern, altered only in certain details at the discretion of the priest. In the outlook, spirit, and manner of his interpretation of the liturgy, he was answerable to no one. Any challenge to his decisions was regarded either as a personal attack on him, or as disloyalty to the Church. Such an atmosphere was hardly conducive to honest and constructive discussion between clergy and people.

On the other hand, today we cannot go to the other extreme and allow every individual in the congregation to demand that his wishes be followed. If the manner of worshipping is open to constant criticism from every quarter, its elevated character will soon be lost. No one can put his heart into a prayer if he knows that immediately after church some of the more clever members of the congregation are going to tear to pieces the theology, form, and diction of the prayer.

Followers of the Liturgical Movement believe that this kind of problem can be solved, and in many places is solved, by restoring a proper theological climate to the Church. Jesus Christ is King of Kings and our great High Priest. Sanctified by the Holy Spirit, Christians are made sharers in this royal priesthood of Christ.[8] Individually and collectively the people of a parish have not only the right but the duty to assume responsibility for the worship they offer. They must understand what the liturgy means so that when it is performed it may be offered to God with their conscious and rational endorsement. Only thus can we speak of "a reasonable, holy, and living sacrifice." In other words, we do not worship as cattle, but as men, women, and children who were created for freedom as the sons and daughters of God and as the brothers and sisters of Jesus Christ. This royal and priestly community, moreover, is not a chaotic mob. It is characterized by the unity and order of the household of God. This unity and order are upheld by the pastor who has been *ordained* for precisely this purpose. As a presbyter[9] and as the commissioned representative of the Bishop, it is his function to preside over the local assembly of the priestly people. His liturgical presidency is exactly analogous to his presidency in other aspects of parish life.[10] He may himself have many talents or few, but as president he will strive to see that the talents of his people are evoked and utilized. As *sacerdos*[11] he will seek to have all of these talents—his own and his people's—offered to God through Christ, "being sanctified by the Holy Ghost." [12]

In the atmosphere established by this kind of theology, frank discussion of worship, and of other activities in the parish, not only becomes possible, but is recognized as imperative. When liturgy is seen as the corporate activity of the parish, then existing practices can be criticized without the appearance of a personal attack on the rector or his assisting clergy. When his presidential role is understood, he can listen to the proposals of others without appearing to abdicate his own leadership. When people have come to a conscious awareness of the royal priesthood in which they too share, they can talk about their liturgy, disrobe it, and even dissect it, without ceasing to respect and honor it. Here, as in many other matters, we learn something of what is meant by our freedom of access in Christ. Such an approach is quite impossible, however, if people do not love the liturgy. The liturgy is hard to love if people see it conducted week after week in a dull and lifeless manner, without feeling, without imagination, and without joy. In the past, this is exactly what too many people have been exposed to.

Spiritual liberation naturally leads to an unfettering of worship, and uninhibited participation in worship naturally encourages a sense of spiritual freedom. One of the interesting surprises of the liturgical movement in Anglicanism has been the flexibility and spontaneity in the celebration of the Eucharist which appears as people experience the reality of Christian renewal. Cheerless, gloomy churches discover what it is to keep festivals with the sound of trumpets and bells, the glow of bright colors, and the laughter of children. Inhibited, fearful folk discover the happiness of coming to the Lord's Table with people of other cultural and racial backgrounds. And some of us, who most love the music and ceremony of solemn worship, have also discovered what it is to kneel around an ordinary table in a house, while a priest in ordinary clothes, with a slice of good brown bread and a glass of red wine, celebrates the Mysteries of the New Covenant.[13] When Christians know that the living Christ is really present, they do not need to be afraid to pray or to sing, to smile or to cry, or to join hands with fellow-worshippers. Christ, the full, complete, and perfect Man, comes to us, to share His perfect humanity with us. At His altar, if nowhere else, men, women, and children can experience without shame the joy of being people.

The Future Renewal of Theology

The foregoing observations and comments may give the reader an impression of how many followers of the Liturgical Movement approach the theoretical and practical questions that arise in the conjunction of worship and teaching. In its decades of increasing growth and influence, this movement retains its conviction that Christian people, when allowed to exercise their royal priesthood in Christ, can make wise decisions. Likewise, they can exercise a creative and sacrificial Christian witness in their church, in their homes, in their daily work, in their social relationships, and in other aspects of life. As we see it, it is the function of theology to provide the reasonable, intellectual framework within which people can experience this renewal and this liberation of the Gospel, and can give this experience a constructive relationship to the whole of life. Accordingly we believe that theological seminaries would be better occupied if they devoted more of their time to imparting theology to the laity, and utilized modern methods of communicating it to a wide section of the Christian public. Ultimately, for economic and other reasons, they will see the desirability of doing so. Hence, followers of the Liturgical Movement envisage in the long run a considerable readjustment of the scope and character of religious training at both the elementary and the more advanced levels. An important facet of this readjustment is the encouragement of priests and deacons who have not had seminary training and who, after ordination, continue to support themselves in secular trades and professions.[14] In many parts of the world today, and within certain sections of American society, such an arrangement is the only reasonable means of continuing the administration of the rites and sacraments of the Church. A "self-supporting ministry" is intellectually quite acceptable if the priestly character of the whole congregation is seen as its context, and if the Church is willing to impart its theology, in a simple, popular manner, to its people as a whole.

With such prospects in view, followers of the Liturgical Movement believe that the future for Christian education is exciting. Although this movement commands the allegiance of many scholars, it remains committed to a fundamentally popular and democratic conception of education. The basic elements of Christian theology can be learned by virtually any believer, and the Church must not be allowed to have a clear conscience until it has presented these truths to its people at large. In the renewal of theological teaching, liturgy can play a crucial role. For it is in the liturgy that lay people can offer all aspects of their lay lives in the world to the Creator of the world. In the liturgy this offering is made through the hands of Jesus Christ—King, High Priest, Carpenter, and Man among men. In the liturgy this offering is consecrated by the Holy Spirit, who is Himself the Breath of Life, and who makes all things new.

11

CHANGING SOCIAL STRUCTURES AND THE CHURCH'S EDUCATIONAL TASK

BY *Alden D. Kelley*

EVERY aspect of education is confronted today with the problem of social change. The structures and institutions of society are universally, not just in America but in every country of the world, going through a period of "rapid social change." This seems to be not merely a phase but an enduring characteristic that can be projected into the indefinite future. It is more than rapid; it is accelerating and radical, a global revolution.

As pointed out by Emmanuel G. Mesthene, executive director of the Harvard University Program on Technology and Society,[1] we have for centuries been followers of the ancient Greek philosopher Parmenides, the apostle of the permanent, the stable, and the eternal, who argued that change is illusory, transitory, and imperfect. Now we have moved into a "Heraclitean" age. Heraclitus saw reality as flux and change and dismissed the permanent as unreal and imperfect. This has posed a dilemma for the institutions of education because by their very nature they are communicators of the treasures of the past and indoctrinators and interpreters of the social values of their time. How will the educational enterprise organize itself to help men be at home in a world of constant change? Even the most advanced programs of scientific and technological training are likely to turn out graduates with skills and competences that will be obsolete in five years or less.

Educators are generally within the stream of "intellectuals" who as a group are the main representatives of the cultural enclave that has emphasized individualism against collectivism, agrarianism versus urbanism, social homogeneity versus heterogeneity. This tradition is particularly deep-rooted in America. It was Thomas Jefferson who remarked that "the mobs of great cities add just so much to the support of pure government, as sores do to the strength of the human body" and "I view great cities as pestilential to the morals, the health, and the liberties of man." [2]

Anything that can be said about the innate conservatism of the educational establishment can be repeated and raised to another power, as descriptive of the churches. They are committed, by and large, to the "eternal verities," to an unchanging absolute, to a reality remote and detached from the hustle and bustle of the world. This "mighty fortress" (Ein' feste burg) slant ignores, of course, their primal vision of a God operative in history and involved in day to day events. Sadly, much of the popular appeal of the churches today is to those who would flee from the dynamics of the present world and find a refuge for themselves and a reinforcement of their yearning for stability within the citadel churches, within the walls of a religious sanctuary. Here one may escape from the "changes and chances of this mortal life," [3] it is thought.

The churches, however, like schools, colleges, and universities are not wholly exempt from the social revolution of our time because, sociologically speaking, they are "dependent variables," *i.e.*, as a part of a larger social context their continuation, indeed their growth, depends on their adaptability, conscious or otherwise, to their environment. Their frantic efforts to be "relevant" to the time and place testify to at least an unconscious recognition of the forces for change within ecclesiastical institutions and theological thought. All too often, however, the restructuring of Church life is unplanned, undesired, unconscious, and insignificant ("unauthentic"). Thus, far from being a determinative ingredient in the ferment (yeast that leavens the loaf or, again in sociological terms, "an independent variable"), they give the impression of being but one of the gaseous bubbles on the surface.

It is not difficult to appreciate, then, why the traditional and institutionalized churches are not competent for "the equipment of the saints for the work of the ministry" [4] in a changing world.

When we consider the Church school as one sector of the educational task of the churches, we see a confluence of the built-in staticism of both the educational and the religious establishments. At precisely this point, conservatism is compounded and raised to the *nth* degree. The average Church school teacher and the general run of Church educational programs, with some notable exceptions perhaps, are completely futile and irrelevant to the world of change in which we live. Nothing could be better calculated to unfit children, adolescents, and adults for the Christian life in today's dynamic society. The underlying assumptions of teachers and curricula seem to be an eighteenth-century pietism in a nineteenth-century agrarian culture characterized by a cozy community of stable "primary relationships." Such a world, if it ever existed except in some ideal never-never land, is evaporating with astonishing speed.

One last point, by way of introduction, should be made. Although the concern here is with changing social structures, it must not be overlooked that on a deeper level what is happening is changing humanity. There is being revealed to us a "new man," unlike any of his forebears.[5] Men are not only the creators of culture in the sense that culture is a humanly contrived "secondary environment" imposed on the primary environment, nature, but also, the creatures of the culture in which they live. In fact, the cultural (technological) achievements of man in this epoch are so vast that the primary environment is being significantly altered: space exploration, medical advances, land productivity, instantaneous communication, climate control, the growth of metropolitan areas, etc., on one hand and, on the other hand, nuclear fall-out, pollution of water and air, the population explosion, and the depletion of natural resources such as petroleum, forests, agricultural lands, and minerals are among the many dysgenic elements in contemporary life. All this, and more, adds up to the gradual transformation of the human species—biologically, psychologically, sociologically, and religiously. Thus, the additional question for the educational enterprise of the Church is: Is it prepared to cope not only with the changing social structures but with "man come of age"? Or, again: Can the churches recognize, cooperate with, and challenge, where necessary, the world as the arena of God's activity?

The New Creation

The complexity of the social revolution makes impossible the ranking of primary, secondary, tertiary factors. All the multivarious elements that characterize the present era are interdependent and, in fact, operate to catalyze each other. Hence, the effort to sort out the "prime movers," the "catalysts," and the "inhibitors," as undertaken by Egbert De Vries,[6] is not particularly helpful and is, indeed, highly debatable.

However, one must begin somewhere so, without commitment to doctrinaire Marxism, first to be mentioned is the highly visible and all pervasive industrialization of contemporary culture. This permeates the whole of our economic life and even where not much advanced is the goal of those emerging nations whose economies are relatively unrationalized. Too often the first step after formal independence by former colonial territories is to secure a modern steel mill, a petro-chemical factory, or a hydro-electric dam (along with its own national, usually subsidized, airline). Such are not mere status symbols but regarded as necessary counters in the game.

But industrialization has moved swiftly from the era of steam, largely dependent on manpower, through electric power to the technically sophisticated processes of automation and cybernation. This revolution has not been only in the area of manufacturing and processing but has involved also research, invention, transportation, and communication. It now embraces supervision and control of manufacturing, sales, and accounts at one end of the scale and mechanization of agriculture at the other end. Farms, forests, etc., are today like mines or oil wells: raw material producing factories. This is enough of a reminder of the almost incredible scientific and technological achievements of recent decades and of the nearly unlimited promise for the future. It suggests that no aspect of human living—economics, politics, family life, community affairs, education, religion and morals—is uninfluenced by the technological "great leap forward." It would be expected, also, that such powerful forces would find their embodiment, institutionalization, in appropriately new forms of social organization.

By and large, this expectation has been, or is in the process of being, fulfilled. The characteristic community expression is urbanization, the rapid growth of metropolitan life. Cities, even large cities, are not a new phenomenon; they go back five or six thousand years. But in ancient times their influence was mostly political and military, not cultural; those who lived outside, and the bulk of the world's population did, were not especially affected.

But, consider the growth of population centers in the United States in less than two hundred years. The Federal census counts any center of 2500 population as a city. In 1775 only five per cent of the population lived in areas of 2500 or above; there was no city of over 50,000 population. By 1920 over half of the country's population lived in cities; by 1930, fifty per cent were in cities of 100,000; by 1960, sixty per cent lived in metropolises ("SMSA" means "Standard Metropolitan Statistical Areas" of 200,000 or more, as defined in 1963); there are listed, moreover, twenty-four areas of more than one million population.

Put another way, there were in 1960 fifteen times as many rural communities (non-city, *i.e.*, less than 2500) as in 1790, but there were 420 times as many urban people. By 1960 the farm population was down to fifteen per cent of the total (compared with ninety-five per cent in 1790). The projected growth of metropolitan areas, by some, is that by A.D. 2000, ninety-eight per cent of the population will be urban.

America is not exceptional in this respect. Great Britain, Germany, and the Benelux countries of Europe are proportionately more urbanized than the U.S.A. Also, this is a worldwide phenomenon: the cities of Africa, Asia (Tokyo is the largest city in the world and has over ten per cent of the total Japanese population of nearly one hundred million), and the Australian-New Zealand territories have had a fantastic growth in the past twenty years. Urbanization like technological industrialization is almost universal.

It is a mistake, however, to regard urbanization as merely a matter of area and population statistics. As a cultural change it penetrates even the most remote villages and hamlets. We are shifting from a predominantly agrarian or small town culture to an urbanized one. The urban sprawl is most dramatically evident if one flies at night from Milwaukee around the lower end of the Great Lakes going over Chicago, Gary, Toledo, Cleveland, Erie, Buffalo, etc., or from Portland, Maine, down the Atlantic Coast to Richmond, Virginia—on either route the street lights are almost continuous.

Moreover, the small towns are themselves within the commercial and communication orbits of the metropolitan areas.[7] Urbanization, therefore, should refer to

> a structure of common life in which diversity and the disintegration of tradition are paramount. It means a type of impersonality in which functional relations multiply. It means that a degree of tolerance and anonymity replace moral sanctions and long-term acquaintanceships. The urban center is the place of human control, of rational planning, of bureaucratic organization. . . . It is everywhere.[8]

As such, urbanism is a way of life, a style of living that is *sui generis* to our era. The French philosopher, Maurice Merleau-Ponty has described it as a particular *"manière d'être,"* [9] implying a special *shape* as well as a "style" of being.

Harvey Cox in *The Secular City* endeavors to fill in some of the details of the shape of urban life. He refers particularly to anonymity and mobility. With these may be linked associated characteristics such as anomie and cultural pluralism.

The personal anonymity of urban centers is well known. It issues from the great diversity of personal relations particularly on the secondary and functional level; primary relationships are lacking or restricted in number. In a sense this is a necessary protection for the individual—an instinctive or acquired defense mechanism against overwhelming intrusion into one's personal life. Such is welcomed by many who find a sort of freedom within the "lonely crowd," but others feel lost.

Because of exposure to the great variety of people at many levels of relationships, and the need for tolerance, there results "a reduction of value consensus among those who are now more and more alike in superficial ways." [10] This normlessness, value confusion, is known by sociologists and psychologists as "anomie" or "anomia." The problem for many is increased because within an urban culture there are relatively few influential value-supporting institutions (family, school, church, fraternal organizations, or trade unions). Moreover, some of these are in conflict with one another or individuals are in revolt against the more traditional and older institutions. Hence, in many instances the turning to "subcultures" such as ethnic or "national groups," adolescent gangs, occupational or professional associations, religious sects, or economic organizations (corporations). [11]

Social mobility may be of two types: horizontal and vertical. The former refers to the spatial or geographical movement of people from community to community: the migration from the inner-city to the suburbs, the in-migration from rural areas to the cities, the continuous shuffling of young executives and their families from one part of the country (or even to overseas branches) by the large corporation, the flight of "senior citizens" from the northern temperate zone to more equable climates, etc. American people are constantly on the move.

By "vertical" mobility is meant the movement, generally upward, from social class to social class: lower, lower middle, middle, upper middle, and upper. Although class stratification is not often openly confessed in this country, it is a fact (determined by education, housing areas, type of housing, economic opportunity, occupation, and income source) well-known to sociologists.[12] Vertical social mobility (upward or downward) is one of the most notable features of America[13] and other urbanized countries.

Closely related to the mobility character of an urbanized culture is the other, perhaps obverse, side of the coin—social pluralism. This takes the form of persistence of some social groupings—religious, ethnic, national, etc. Here we have whole cultural communities that for one reason or the other are not assimilated or integrated into the larger social "mix." The functioning of sects and cults among the disprivileged and the place of denominationalism and secularism among the more privileged may be considered examples of religious pluralism.[14]

One other factor in our changing society needs to be mentioned: mass organization. This has become familiar enough in its varied aspects to all of us. Not only is mass production by gigantic industrial corporations an element of our everyday life but the techniques of mass organization, even manipulation, are a commonplace of housing, education, communication, government, and religious bodies.[15] In some degree all of us exhibit the characteristics of the "organization man"; the exceptions seem only to be alcoholics, members of sects such as Jehovah's Witnesses and the Black Muslims, and self-conscious non-conformists (adolescents, "beatniks," etc.). Most of these maintain their "independence" by adherence to a subcultural or contra-cultural group. The privileges and responsibilities of the individual are gradually being eroded: ZIP codes for mail, DDD for the telephone, social security numbers, numbered charge accounts and credit cards, company billings ("Do not fold, staple, or otherwise mutilate this card"), and the IRS forms are all "outward and visible signs of an inward and spiritual" obliteration.[16]

It is natural that within the context of such enormous structures of power—there is no such thing as "the power structure" but, rather, many and diverse centers of power—many should feel overwhelmed, helpless, and often apathetic. "What difference does one person, worker, bystander, or voter make?" they quite properly ask.

There are other characteristics of our present industrial-technological urban culture, probably less central, than those mentioned. But, the foregoing would seem sufficient to indicate in a general way the more notable features of our rapidly changing social order. This is the sort of a world that the Church confronts and of which it is a part. Everything that has been suggested as features of mid-twentieth-century urbanization is applicable not merely to the large metropolitan areas but also to suburbia and rural America because the whole land and its people are going through the same process. It is often forgotten by the critics of the big city that the obvious dysgenic factors of metropolitan life, such as crime, disease, inferior educational facilities, and poor housing, are found in proportion in rural areas, all of which have their slums, inadequate medical facilities,[17] underfinanced and inadequate school systems,[18] and so on. The fundamental structures and functions of American culture are generally quite similar whether one lives in the Consolidated Metropolitan Area of New York (population about fifteen million), on a sheep ranch in Montana, in Seattle, or in an orange grove in Florida.

Up to this point, the discussion would seem to concentrate on the characteristics and functions of contemporary society rather than to deal directly with its structures. However, the structures are the institutional embodiments and carriers of cultural functions. In fact, structures are defined by the way they act or function. Structure (social) is a *general term for all those attributes of social groups and types which make them susceptible of being viewed as composite or complex wholes, made up of interdependent parts.* This is the definition offered by the *Dictionary of Sociology* edited by Henry Pratt Fairchild.[19] Understood in this sense the structures of society include more than the family, the school, the local community or neighborhood, the institutions of industry, commerce, and finance, the churches and other religious groups, and governmental organizations in and of themselves. To be taken into account, also, are the often intangible and informal relationships that characterize their functioning. They are not a bowl of cherries that can be taken out one by one and scrutinized singly; rather, social structures are more like a network or webbed pattern of closely intertwined and interdependent living cellular organisms. Therefore, any consideration of one leads ineluctably to all.

The Learning-Teaching and Serving-Ruling Church in a Secular Society

The Church as a "servant church" requires accepting the terms on which men live; *i.e.,* within the structures in which men live. It cannot be the Church if it is merely just another institution along with other social institutions. It is, of course, one of the institutions within society but it is more.[20]

Hence, the importance of a sociological understanding of the world. As stated by Albert van den Heuvel of the Youth Council of the World Council of Churches:

> Taking the form of a slave means to let the world have its own forms and fill those with the content of the Gospel. Therefore sociology is essential for the Church—it is not helpful, it is essential. Without it we cannot renew our structures. It describes the house in which the slave lives." [21]

This means we must take seriously the phrase, now so popular, "holy worldliness" so that we recognize God's presence and activity in the "secular." Because the Bible and the Christ esteem the secular, the Church itself must be secular. It has been said many times before, even by this author, but, apparently, it cannot be repeated too often, that the "secular," "secularity," and "secularization" (as a process) are *not* to be confused with *secularism.* Any "ism," even humanism or theism, must be rejected by the Christian because it represents the absolutization of a single principle or concept and substitutes it for God. "Isms" are demonic and forms of idolatry.

But the secular as descriptive of *this* world and its processes as the sphere of God's creative and redemptive activity is firmly rooted in the "Holy Scriptures [which] contain all Doctrine required as necessary for eternal salvation through faith in Jesus Christ." [22] It is meaningless to say, "Let the Church be the Church" unless this implies an appreciation of the fact that the Church is only the Church when it is servant, a slave (perhaps rejected as was its Master) of and in the secular order.

If this understanding of the Church has any validity, then our vision of the educational task of the Church is radically (literally going to the root of the matter) altered.

Not only, as suggested above, is much of the educational

approach of the Church hopelessly irrelevant to the contemporary social revolution, but the self-understanding, or
self image, of the Church as a teaching institution is false.

It is common in the Roman Church to make a distinction
between the "teaching Church" (*ecclesia docens*) and the
"learning Church" (*ecclesia discens*). The former role is
that of the hierarchy and the latter role is assigned to the
ordinary laymen, the men and women in the pew. What is
required at the present time is the recognition that the
Church, as servant or slave, is throughout, from top to bot-
tom the "learning Church"; no exceptions even among "professional theologians."

For centuries—and the Reformation did nothing to modify the situation but rather heightened and solidified the
tradition by a spate of catechisms, theses, edicts, and confessions—the Church has operated as if it had all the answers. This is to say that its educational task is not to provide answers but to ask questions and more questions. Kierke-
gaard saw this in his deliberate adoption of Socrates as the
paradigm of the Christian preacher and teacher.

At the same time, we must not overlook the fact that
the Gospel is news, good news, a proclamation (*kerygma*)
and that the long prophetic tradition of the Old Israel and
the New Israel was grounded in speaking with authority—
"thus saith the Lord." But, the preaching of the Gospel was
and is, if it is *the* Gospel, to men where they are and in
acceptance of who they are and where they live. This means
witnessing and serving that is directly related to people in
their real needs, conscious or not, and within the structures
in which they live, move, and have their being. It is helping
people to be open to God and not to be closed to the world,
because there, indeed, is where God is.

Such a view raises embarrassing, even humiliating, questions for our customary Church practices—in preaching,

liturgy, teaching, organization, and the structuring of Church life (including the ministry), and the relation of all these to the socio-cultural revolution through which we are going. One can understand and sympathize with those Church people (clergy and laity) who find the tensions intolerable and would return to the catacombs, where Christians might withdraw "from the centers of influence, a reversion to the position of primitive Christians, who were simply responsible to power not for it."[23]

On the other hand, the Church does have a real place in society, other than being an obsequious lackey, which is what some envisage being a servant means, if it is to avoid being pushed to the periphery of personal and social life and escape from being "ghetto" Christianity. The churches must confront honestly and courageously the social realities of our time. On the whole, as stated by Gayraud S. Wilmore, it

> has demonstrated a naive and moralistic approach. . . . It has assumed that if it eschewed power its "social concern" would have an educative influence and its massive institutional baggage would at least not give either side of a struggle an advantage as long as it remained a "nonpolitical" factor in the social order. It has been wrong on both counts.[24]

Dr. Wilmore goes on to write:

> It is not a matter of the church's trying to do what political parties and great corporations are better equipped to do. That would be both impossible and undesirable. It is simply a matter of the church's doing what is possible for it in each situation; to use faithfully that modicum of power it can generate and call a halt to the retreat from the firing line and the pious pretension that God works only through the weak and powerless.[25]

This candid recognition of the Church as one center of power in the constellation of power structures (the Church as "ruling") cannot be denied simply on the ground that too often the Church and its influence are conspicuous by their absence.

How, then, can we approach the education and training of Christians so that they may live both as servants of the world and heirs and sons[26] of the time?

An Unscientific Postscript on Christian Education Today

Probably no one less qualified to comment on the Church school and its program, as it has been and is today operative, could have been chosen than the writer. One third of my ministry was spent in ministering to college and university students and the remainder in teaching in theological schools. Accordingly, direct experience with formal Christian education of the young is lacking. However, perhaps for that very reason there has been developed a sensitivity to its inadequacies. So far as understanding how one as a Christian and member of the Church lives, witnesses, and serves in the contemporary world is concerned, the results seem unimpressive.

If not almost wholly ignorant of the significance of Christianity in the world today, of the nature of the rapidly changing social structures, of their *ministry* as members of the People of God, so-called "good and well-trained" Churchmen (young adults) have been either wholly preoccupied with the institutional, financial, and social functions of the Church or obsessively devoted to the minutiae of ecclesiastical millinery and/or the manicuring of their morals. It rarely dawns on them that *they* are the Church, that *they* are the ministry.

Let there be no misunderstanding at this point. This is

not so much a criticism of the failure of other "holy men in round collars" as a personal confession of the inability to carry out my conviction, well expressed by Hans Ruedi Weber of the Department of the Laity of the World Council of Churches: "The laity are not the helpers of the clergy so that the clergy can do their job, but the clergy are helpers of the whole people of God, so that the laity can be the Church." [27]

This seems to me to require an almost complete reversal of the goals and general orientation of Christian education material and methods. The task is not how to train children and adults for life in the Church, as the "gathered" church or "manifest" church (Paul Tillich) but for life in the world, the "dispersed" church or the "latent" church (Paul Tillich). This means beginning not so much with the literary and historical legacies of Christianity (Bible, Church history, liturgy, etc.) as with the booming, buzzing world in which we live. (For youngsters who are still living within the more or less cloistered atmosphere of "nice" families, "respectable" suburbs, and "good" schools, this may mean establishing contact with them at the point of their own experience, problems, and difficulties.) One can assert with confidence, however, that it is possible, although not always easy, to move from where people are to where God calls them. In so doing, the traditional, and by no means obsolete, ways of the Church and style of Christian life can become meaningful.

Even in the suburbs where the churches have seemed to be most "successful" and "relevant" (but, probably, irrelevant to God and His purposes), there is no real escape from the social revolution. As Daisuke Kitagawa has pointed out, the lily-white suburbs are not exempt from the problems of racism.[28] So they are also exposed and vulnerable to the total cultural revolution—industrial, technological, urban, etc.[29]

Perhaps those in Christian education need to take a leaf from the book of the public education enterprise and adopt a supplementary or "enriched" curriculum. Or, it may be that what is needed is the ecclesiastical equivalent of *Operation Headstart*[30] (not just in the metropolitan centers but in the protected suburbs and the rural areas). It could be called *Operation Catch Up*.

12

CHRISTIAN EDUCATION IN CONFRONTATION WITH WORLD RELIGIONS

BY *Lee A. Belford*

MODERN technology has virtually annihilated distance. With the constant shrinking of the world a confrontation of the world's religions is a fact which can become increasingly more critical in its implications for world understanding and peace. The problem is especially significant for the Christian who was brought up on the assumption that his religion by its own virtue was destined to embrace the world so that religiously we would all be one. The predominance of Christianity and even the validity of its other claims are now seriously questioned. Scarcely one-third of the world's population professes to be Christian and the ratio is decreasing, due primarily to the population explosion in non-Christian areas of the world, but due also to the renascence of many of the old religions which were long quiescent. India has produced many able apologists for a

182

revitalized Hinduism. Buddhism in Southeast Asia is often identified with national loyalty, but there is also a rejuvenation and a self-conscious appreciation of Buddhism's virtues. Muslim missionaries have staked out North and Central Africa as their domain and not only Christian missionaries but Christians in general are often forced to live and work under severe limitations. No longer is it expected that a non-Christian will be embarrassed and reticent about his beliefs. A sense of pride is clearly evident. The problem is how to keep a variety of dynamic and viable religions from becoming such a divisive force that world understanding, cooperation, and unity are impeded.

A World of Interacting Persons

If God is truly Lord of the universe, then God is at work in creating one world of interacting persons. The increasing awareness of the scope of God's dominion, beginning with tribalism and moving to universalism, is a story well told in the Bible. Amos proclaimed that the neighboring nations were ruled by God; Jeremiah fought a narrow nationalism; Deutero-Isaiah insisted on God's universal concern; and that was the concern of Jesus.

The Christian is in Christ and shares His ministry of reconciliation. It is a ministry that involves reconciling Christians and non-Christians for the sake of the wholeness of mankind. If a Christian's religion is meaningful to him, it is natural that he should wish to share his beliefs. However, conversion is secondary to respect for a person, including his beliefs that differ from one's own. The non-Christian does not become a child of God by conversion; he is already a child of God. Because, according to Christian belief, Christ incorporates humanity in His person, a person should be able to look into the eyes of a stranger and see Christ there. We are already in Christ; we are already brothers. The practice of brotherhood begins with the neighbor next door; it does not end there. Its horizons are limited only by the size of the universe. The Christian has a mission of service, a mission for people, to people, and with people of all nations, races, and creeds. His mission is to demonstrate by thought, word, and deed that God can reconcile and renew men and society. Such a reconciliation and renewal cannot be achieved if human dignity and respect are denied others. If men take their religion seriously, then their beliefs cannot be treated as mere oddities. They must be taken seriously.

Recently The Society for the Propagation of the Gospel gathered together a hundred or so of its new missionary candidates to listen to addresses given by representatives of the Buddhist, Muslim, Hindu, and Jewish religions. Missionary mission is a two-way street. If you are prepared to give, you must be prepared to receive. Even though the Christian believes that God entered into a covenant relationship with Israel and that the Christian Church is the new Israel, the Christian also affirms that God may speak through any and all peoples, any and all institutions. Approached from the other perspective, the awareness of the ultimate is not denied *ipso facto* to any people anywhere.

John Macquarrie has summarized the biblical view in cogent fashion:

> The Synoptic Gospels, explicitly or implicitly, stress the unique authority of our Lord, but they could hardly be said to make an exclusive claim, even in the famous but hotly debated passage declaring that "no one knows the Father except the Son and any to whom the Son chooses to reveal him." The Fourth Gospel speaks of the Word that has been in the world from the beginning and that in some sense enlightens every man, yet it speaks also of the "only-begot-

ten" Son and claims that no one comes to the Father except through him. Acts represents St. Peter as maintaining that "there is salvation in no one else" except Christ, but St. Paul is represented as finding some common ground between the gospel which he preaches and the beliefs of the Athenians. It has been vigorously disputed whether in the early chapters of Romans St. Paul recognizes a natural theology or not —perhaps the rival exegeses here have been considerably influenced by the theological preferences of the exegetes. The writer of Hebrews certainly thinks of Jesus as the "author and finisher" of our faith, yet the history of faith is traced back not only to Hebrew patriarchs but to Noah and other mythical figures who belong to the whole human race.[1]

It should not be inferred that Christianity should give up all claim to uniqueness in the name of an open-minded attitude toward all religions. To say that all religions in every aspect are equally true and good is to deny the meaning of truth and goodness. Differences do exist. The moment it is claimed that all religions are basically the same, true dialogue becomes an impossibility, for dialogue is possible only where there are differences in standpoint. There is inevitably a degree of tension between one's commitment to his own religious beliefs and an openness to the religious beliefs of others. This tension can never be completely eliminated, nor is it desirable that it should be, but it can be alleviated if a spirit of reverence for the convictions of others can be preserved. Archbishop William Temple openly averred that the virtue of comparative religion is that it brings men to a genuine reverence for other men's beliefs. It certainly opens up such possibilities although in some instances the beliefs of others have been treated with such disparagement that little reverence emerged. Of course, beliefs that are important enough to determine the nature of one's life deserve the respect of others. The spirit of reverence displayed by anyone deserves the reverence of others and thus there should be a reverence for reverence.

The ecumenical movement was motivated partially by a realization of the inadequacies of many of our institutions in the face of a growing secularism. There was also the recognition that a lowering of the barriers that separate Christians and the achievement of a greater degree of cooperation and unity is according to God's will. Now Christians must recognize that God is calling for greater concord among the religions of the world.

The Approach to Other Religions

If it is acknowledged that a confrontation of Christianity with other religions is not only inevitable but highly desirable, the next question concerns the approach to be followed. For purposes of clarification, a review of principles or approaches is in order.

In viewing the religions of the world one may assume the posture of an observer or a participant. The observer claims that he is able to view all religions with equal detachment. He boasts of his lack of commitment. He does not feel "spoken to" by any transcending force nor does he have any commitment to ultimate reality in religious terms. He can be tolerant of all religions because no religion makes any significant difference to him. He can be positive in his attitude in the sense that he assumes that religion in general, whatever it is, is good for those who like it, or he can be negative in attitude, assuming that religious ideas are outmoded, the product of ignorance, and the result of a cultural lag. Note that the observer makes certain assumptions—he does not probe or explore. He is merely a dilettante with a superficiality that has nothing to do with confrontation.

On the other hand, the role of observer is a fit one for a

nation. Whether it is good for a nation's attitude to be positive or negative is a point open to debate. The attitude of the government of the United States toward religion is positive. The pledge to the flag incorporates the words "one nation, under God"; the national motto is "In God we trust"; the motto is inscribed on coins and currency; tax exemption is granted to churches and other religious institutions; and clergymen are given special consideration such as exemption from military service. No religion is singled out for special support because the government assumes the posture of neutrality. Neither God nor any other religious term is defined and the very definition of what constitutes a religion is phrased as broadly as possible. The Ethical Culture Society has no creed. Some of its leaders are philosophical naturalists who deny the supernatural completely yet the Society enjoys tax privileges as a religious institution. The same privileges are extended to an avowedly atheistic American Buddhist society. Queen Elizabeth I of England once remarked that she was not interested in making windows in people's minds to see what they believed. The same is true of the government of the United States. It is not concerned with seeing or evaluating what is going on in people's minds in regard to their religious beliefs.

The attitude of the Soviet government toward religion is basically negative. It makes no differentiation among the beliefs of Eastern Orthodox, Roman Catholic, or Evangelical Protestant Christians or the beliefs of Muslims and Jews. The whole vocabulary, including the very word religion, has bad connotations. There is no consideration of religious beliefs in depth and basically no religious persecution.

Although some countries have state religions and give preference and even support to one denomination of a religion in preference to all others, with the loss of homogeneity through international exchange, the role of observer

will have to be increasingly assumed. Where there are conflicting and competing groups there is no alternative. The
same can be said of the United Nations and other international groups of a similar nature.

In regard to individuals, if religion does not involve commitment, then it cannot be seriously divisive, any more than
the odor of a perfume can be basically divisive. It is only
where there are deep religious convictions that deep conflicts occur. If a person is to be detached in regard to
religion, if he is to be merely an observer, no problem arises
in regard to inter-religious understanding.

The second position that a person can occupy in regard
to religion is that of a participant. Those who take confrontation among the world's religions seriously, though
admittedly with different degrees of involvement, may be
placed in five categories. There are:

1. Those who seek unity by reduction of beliefs to a common denominator.
2. Those who have a hidden assumption in seeking unity
   among religions.
3. Those who approach other religions from the standpoint that their religion is the sole custodian of the
   truth and evaluate all other religions accordingly.
4. Those who seek a knowledge of all religions for the
   sake of finding new insights out of which a new and
   higher religion than any of the existing religions may
   emerge.
5. Those who are firmly committed to the fundamentals
   of their religion but yet are open to new insights
   through contact with other religions.

The language of those in categories (1) and (2) often
merges. The spokesmen for both groups often seem to be
saying the same thing although the differences are real.
Those in category (3) react against the reductionism of (1)

and the hidden assumptions of (2), especially if they are unacceptable assumptions. There are many points of similarity between those in categories (4) and (5) as will become apparent. Category (4) is often closely related to category (2) since there are often hidden assumptions and those in category (5) are often closely related to those in category (3) inasmuch as certain fundamentals of belief are asserted at the outset. It is category (5) which offers the most significant approach to inter-religious confrontation.

A Common Denominator

(1) *There are those who seek unity by reduction of beliefs to a common denominator.* If you begin with an element all religions have in common and discard all differences, then there must necessarily be unity among the religions. Actually the situation is tautological since the conclusion rests in the predicate and is therefore foregone.

This approach can be illustrated by reference to moral laws. Jews, Christians, and Muslims accept the Old Testament of the Bible. Within the Old Testament are found the Ten Commandments. Among them are the following: Honor your father and mother; do not murder; do not commit adultery; do not steal; do not bear false witness; do not covet. These commandments are found associated with every religion. The reason is simple. You cannot have a healthy society unless there is some regard for the sanctity of the family, the primary social institution in every society. You cannot have a healthy society if people murder each other indiscriminately. There must be a regard for truth and a man's greed must be bridled if men are to live in peace. However, some religions are merely tangentially concerned with ethics and support norms of behavior such as these only as the religions are indirectly supportive of a culture, while some religions like the biblical religions have an ethical concern built into their very structure. In spite of the different emphases given to these "laws," it is possible to say that they exist in relation to every religion, and to the extent that the essence of all religions is reduced to their enumeration, it can be said that all religions are basically the same.

The law of reciprocity (the Golden Rule in positive form; the Silver Rule in negative form) is likewise associated with most religions. Reduce the essence of all religions to the concept of reciprocity and unity is found.

Add to the process of reductionism a large amount of obfuscation and it is easy to find a unity in religious terms. With the possible exception of Hinayana Buddhism every major religion has some concept that can be roughly translated "god." By ignoring the vast differences in meaning associated with the word and by relying on English translations, it is possible to say that all major religions with the possible exception cited, believe in God. The same trick can be played with the word "immortality" even though there are differences between Hinduism and Buddhism and a radical difference between them and the biblical concept of the resurrection of the body. There is no end to the extent that one can play with words like this. Whether such a game does anything other than confuse is highly questionable.

A Common Core

(2) *There are those who have a hidden assumption as they seek unity among the religions.* Aldous Huxley deals at length with what he calls the "perennial philosophy." [2] He cites Muslim sufis, Christian mystics, and Hindu philosophers to show that they have a common core. Of course

they do for he has used as his sources the writings of mystics and has found what by definition he set out to find. W. T. Stace describes religion as "the hunger for the non-being which yet is." [3] For him religion is the attempt to get beyond the ordinary world of experience and thought to the ultimate Being which is Non-Being. He feels that biblical references to God as personal, righteous, and loving are only concessions to the plain man and do not represent what is really true.

Huxley and Stace are seeking the common core of religion through a type of mysticism that is central for Vedanta Hinduism. Mysticism does not represent the heart and core of Christianity. It is marginal although there have been some Christian mystics; it is not central for Islam where mysticism is limited primarily to the Sufis.

It may seem as if the assumptions of Huxley and Stace are quite overt and therefore that they belong in category (1) although in their thought they are more sophisticated than many of the spokesmen in category (1). Yet it seems proper to place them in category (2) because some may not be aware that their definition of religion is a very one-sided one. In the final analysis they describe the essence of religion as an awareness of reality which is inexpressible. Reality is inaccessible through the senses or the intellect, indescribable in any of the terms and categories at the command of ordinary language and consciousness, and ultimately approachable only in and through a state of ecstasy which transcends every form and activity. In this ecstasy all sense of separateness, apartness, and difference of the self from the nature of the real disappears. Self-consciousness is obliterated. The individual is either actually merged and made one with the really real or engrossed in a beatific vision of it in which the distinction between subject and object is no longer experienced.

One becomes accustomed to hear Hindus say that all religions are basically the same. In the chapel of The Vedanta Society in New York City there is an inscription from the Vedas inscribed on a wall with the appropriate symbols of the world's great religions, "Truth is one though men call it variously." At the Ramakrishna-Vivekananda Center one encounters a statue of the Buddha at the entrance, a bust of Ramakrishna on the table in the front, and a large reproduction of the Blessed Virgin Mary and the Child Jesus from Raphael's Madonna of the Chair on the north wall. The Hindus delight Christians when they proclaim that Jesus is truly divine; they embarrass Jews when they say that Moses was an incarnation of God. The swamis say that you do not cease to be a Jew or a Christian if you become a Hindu since all religions are equally true. They even say that you can become a better Christian or Jew if you accept Vedanta, the philosophic monism of Hinduism. Here the underlying assumption is that a man becomes a better Christian or Jew only if he gives up the peculiarities of his religion and becomes a Hindu. The Hindu accepts a cyclical interpretation of history and believes that what once happened is bound to happen again. Thus there are many incarnations of God, not just one. The Christian accepts a lineal concept of history, a history that never repeats itself, a history with a beginning, middle, and end. For the Christian there can be only one Incarnation and with it only one Atonement. The Hindu and Christian positions are incompatible and therefore one does not become a better Christian by accepting Vedanta Hinduism—he gives up his Christianity.

One difficulty with postures (1) and (2) is that when you reduce the essence of all religions to a common denominator or use an assumption from one religion as the heart of all religions, there is no way to deal with the differences that appear when there is an actual confrontation between religions. The myths and symbols of a religion, the ceremonies and practices, the customs and traditions do make a difference. Admittedly some of them are purely products of a cultural milieu and need re-examination. To re-examine them is to acknowledge their existence, not to ignore them or dismiss them out of hand as if completely irrelevant.

Exclusiveness

(3) *There are those who approach other religions from the standpoint that their religion is the sole custodian of the truth and evaluate all other religions accordingly.* This is the posture of the religious fanatic who, believing that his religion possesses the sole key to salvation, views all other religions with disparagement, contempt, and at times hatred. Fanaticism is responsible for most of the religious persecution that has resulted from confrontation among religions. Frightened by the idea that God is speaking and working through all peoples, some Christians look for an impregnable defense in biblical infallibility and cite the Bible as the exclusive repository of God's revelation. However, as John Macquarrie points out, Karl Barth has an exclusive christo-centrism and some of his disciples have gone so far as to say that if anyone recognizes other sources of revelation besides Christ, he does not belong to the Christian Church. At one time Emil Brunner also contended that salvation comes only through Christ although it must be admitted that such a statement is capable of broad interpretation. Even though the Christian should rejoice that God's knowledge is not limited to Christians, some Christians still weep at the fact.

The most popular book dealing with comparative religion for a generation was Robert E. Hume's *The World's*

Religions. At the conclusion of his treatment of each religion, he evaluated it, setting forth what he considered the strong and weak points. His criteria were derived basically from Christianity. While evaluation is essential, Hume is placed in this category because he does not probe deeply enough into the religions to ascertain the truths they possess nor is a genuine humility from the Christian stance made clearly evident.

The fanatic serves a useful purpose in his protest against reductionism, but no constructive purpose is served if the best of one's own religion is compared with the worst in all other religions. Basically, the fanatic limits God by destroying his universal sovereignty and in doing so, denies the essential unity of mankind.

An Emergent View

(4) *There are those who seek a knowledge of all re-ligions for the sake of finding new insights out of which a new and higher religion may emerge.* A. N. Whitehead was deeply concerned with the religious quest. He felt that the religious differences that mark the East and the West must be bridged, that deeper meaning must be sought, and that men must be open to a new and synthetic religion that would incorporate the higher values of both traditions.[4] This is also the theme of F. S. C. Northrop.[5] W. E. Hocking places high emphasis upon the changes that have occurred in the world (such as the new internationalism) which force man into a new understanding of God and of man's relationship to Him. Hocking contends that experience alone is real. He maintains that reality is in part a function of the will. He believes that the objects of religious knowledge are in process of development and are responsive in both character and reality to man's will. The idea of God devel-

ops from the community experience and as the community develops through a confrontation of the world's religions, new ideas will develop, according to Hocking.[6]

While Whitehead, Northrop, and Hocking have some relationship to the posture assumed in category (5), the position of Arnold Toynbee is closer to the posture of category (1). Toynbee makes a list of essential truths possessed by seven of the great religions including the statements that the universe is mysterious, there is a presence greater than man himself, man seeks communion with the presence behind phenomena, and the human soul must get rid of its innate self-centeredness. He points out quite cogently how religions in adapting themselves to particular social milieus in time and history acquire aspects of no universal significance. They might be termed accidental accretions. "The message has to be denatured to some extent by a translation of what is permanent and universal into terms of something that is temporal and local."[7] He would like to peel off the temporal and transient characteristics such as theology, the work of intellectuals who merely reflect the thought patterns of their day, self-centeredness in terms of religious exclusiveness, the regard for holy places and rituals regardless of their symbolic value, taboos and social conventions, and myths. The question may well be asked whether reality can be apprehended or intimations of its nature can be conveyed without the use of myths. As for theology, man is bound to formulate his thoughts. When all is said and done, Toynbee does not have much left at the core of religion and he could easily be placed in category (1) except for his real concern with "the" religion of the future to be like no other religion the world has ever known. The position outlined is not his only position but all are similar in his view that present religions are inadequate and we must look forward to a new one.

One of the criticisms of those in this category is that they pull the props from any deep commitment to any religion and offer instead a superficial eclecticism.

Although not advocated by serious scholars, there are those who would synthesize rites and ceremonies and other trappings in a new mixture so that everyone could do things not unrelated to what he is accustomed to doing and yet there would be greater homogeneity. Such a mixture simply would not work.

Openness to New Insights

(5) *There are those who are firmly committed to the fundamentals of their religion and yet are open to new insights through contact with other religions.* They are concerned with the pursuit of truth and the quest for the eternal and therefore there is an openness; yet there is a deep seriousness about their own beliefs and the authentic traditions of their own religious heritage. They reject a relativism that dispenses with the problem of truth, and ultimately of revelation, and yet are eager to investigate other religions to seek the types of experiences that lie behind the expressions of people of diverse cultures. They reject spiritual arrogance which closes the heart and mind and practice genuine humility. They even preserve the possibility of rejecting what is fundamental in their professed religion for either another religion now existing or for the sake of a newly emerging religion. They even reserve the right to reject all religions in the name of an experience of ultimate reality to which no religion does justice.

There is no denying that as a religion develops in a particular society it is affected by geographic and climatic environment, by social organization and economic matters, and by the residue of superstitions, folk-lore, myths, rituals, and customs that sometimes go back to primitive beginnings. With an analysis of other religions a student is given a different frame of reference for evaluating aspects of his own religion. He may find that some of the things he believes and does are merely vestiges of the past that no longer have relevance and he may discover the deeper significance of many of them.

Suppose that a Christian places himself in this category, what may he learn from other religions? He may learn something of tolerance from Hinduism for within Hinduism there is the widest variety of both belief and practice. There is some validity to the conclusion of men like Arnold Toynbee that there cannot be true inter-religious understanding until the Jews, Christians, and Muslims get over the illusion that they are the chosen people and have some very special relationship to God that makes them superior to all other groups.

The Christian affirms his belief in creeds and confessions of faith. He is inclined to believe that his statement of beliefs exhausts the meaning of God. The philosophic Hindu reminds the Christian of God's ultimate indescribability and of man's arrogance in thinking that he can know all about the Ultimate. A creed is more negative than positive since if it were merely positive it would delimit God to the statements made about Him. The Hindu reminds the Christian that religious language is symbolic and that when the Christian speaks of God as Creator of the Heavens and Earth, he is saying that everything has God as its ultimate reference and nothing created is beyond God's domain.

The Christian believes in the Holy Trinity, but the Trinity must always be understood in terms of God's unity. Often Christians destroy the unity in their concern for the three persons. They need Jews and Muslims to remind them that God is one.

The Muslim can remind the Christian of God's majesty and can shame the Christian when he sees how habitually and in relationship to everything a Muslim thinks about God. And the Christian may be humbled by the solidarity of Islam which crosses all racial and ethnic barriers.

From most of the Eastern religions a lesson in meditation can well be learned and a type of spirituality that confers peace and calm in the midst of adversity. These and many other things a Christian can learn provided he is willing to examine other religions with empathy and to subject his own beliefs and behavior patterns to close analysis.

The Christian should always be mindful that Jesus incurred animosity not because of revolutionary teachings— all that he said in the Sermon on the Mount is paralleled in the sayings of ancient rabbis—but because he made drastic evaluations of the religion to which he was born and rejected many customs as irrelevant. Paul dispensed with ritual laws and John demythologized. Christians are guilty today of literalizing myths and holding to symbols that have lost their power. The Holy Spirit works in self-criticism. Therefore the Christian should not be afraid to evaluate his own religion as he evaluates other religions.

A reduction of all religions to a common denominator does not do justice to any religion. Religions must be approached phenomenologically and not in terms of a definition of what religion is. A mixture of aspects of all religions for the sake of one religion would be a hodge-podge without life. For a religion to be real, commitment is essential. The religious fanatic who closes his eyes to another's religious truth and experience and even seeks to exterminate it is at least taking that other religion seriously, which is more than can be said of the reductionists or synthesists. What is needed is both a commitment to a religion experienced in a concrete situation and an openness to all other religions.

In order that there might be dialogue each religion should be loyal to its own heritage. There should be a mutual judging which opens the way to a fair evaluation. There should be self-criticism. The world is moving toward greater unity. The question is whether the religions of the world can respond in creating greater world understanding and brotherhood.

The Christian believes in one God, the Creator of all men and nations. The Christian believes that God has spoken in particular through the Hebrew seers and prophets; that God has revealed Himself in the person of Jesus Christ; that God has spoken and still speaks through the Christian Church. But the Christian dare not deny God the right to speak through the other religions of the world. The Christian must seek the truth wherever it is to be found.

The Christian believes that God is love. He refers to God as Father, father of all human beings. If God is the father of Hindus, Muslims, and people of all religions, then the Christian must love them for God's sake because they are God's beloved. They must be respected as individuals; they must be accorded dignity. What they believe must be taken seriously. They must be listened to as men made in the image of God; and if they are, they may well be instruments through whom God will speak in an age of the confrontation of one religion with another.

13

EDUCATION FOR MISSION

BY *Stephen F. Bayne, Jr.*

I T WOULD seem clear that everything in this chapter must be determined, for the most part, by the way one understands "mission." I find myself generally using the word in two senses. At times, the word refers to the task assigned to a person, group, or whatever. When a new congregation or a new diocese is established somewhere, the clergy and people involved would likely be assigned a measurable job to do. The area, the type and scope of ministry, the expected stages of planning and response—all these would be identified. And it would be proper to use the word "mission" in such a case because it would refer to the sending of people to do a specified job. Certainly this is the sense in which the word is used in military parlance, for the most part; and this is not a bad test of a word.

Alternatively, one sometimes used the word to describe the form of the group to whom responsibility is assigned. The United States of America has a "mission" to the United Nations. In this case, the word is applied to the task-group —a group of people chosen, trained, and assigned their responsibilities in relation to the task to be accomplished.

Certainly the word is used in both those ways about the

Church, and appropriately so. But there is an enormous and explosive enhancement of meaning discovered only when the word is considered theologically, as a word which conceivably could be applied to God. Not all ideas of God could permit the use of such a word about Him. But it is sure that any authentic biblical theology will have at its center an assurance of the dynamic initiative which God takes in His relationships with His creation. Certainly this is supremely characteristic of Christianity, whose theology would be quite senseless if ultimate reality—God—could not be described in terms of dynamic initiative. The God of Christian faith is a God who leads; it is therefore appropriate to speak of those who love Him as His "followers."

At all events, it is characteristic of Christianity to root its understanding of mission, first of all, in God Himself. The Church is indeed sent on a mission; and the form of the Church is dictated by that mission. But both of these undeniable truths depend on a far more radical statement— that the mission is not the Church's, but God's, first of all.

In the pivotal document which gives Anglicans our starting-place, at this period in our history, all of this is said in two simple sentences: "The Church's mission is response to the living God who in His love creates, reveals, judges, redeems, fulfills. It is He who moves through our history to teach and to save, who calls us to receive His love, to learn, to obey and to follow."

If mission be understood this way, then education for mission must surely be shaped so as to prepare the Church and Christian people to identify God's action in the created universe and in our history, and equally to help us to respond to His action in faithful obedience.

Within this hopelessly wide charter, one can isolate at least three areas for particular attention. The first area is that of identifying and understanding God's action in history—the evidence in history of the divine mission. No doubt the core of this exploration is to be found in Holy Scripture; and by the same token the Holy Scripture inescapably becomes the first essential ingredient in missionary education.

Of course we always come to the study of the Bible with extraordinarily mixed motives. Sometimes our aim is nothing more than a kind of devotional housecleaning. Sometimes our curiosity is piqued by a sermon we hear or a book we read. Again we will come to the Bible seeking for the shadow of a mighty rock within a weary land—come wondering whether there are to be found within these books the fixed points we need to orient ourselves.

Of course one could go on indefinitely, describing our mixed motives. But when one thinks about the Holy Scripture, in considering education for mission, one is aware of our particular concern for one thing—how to discern the clues to the divine action in history. "The mighty acts of God" is something of a jargon phrase; I distrust it because so often it is used so as to suggest that the only mighty "acts" are those recorded in Holy Scripture; or alternatively that the mightiest of all the acts are those recorded in Holy Scripture. So in one sense they are. The acts of God in Creation, in Incarnation, and in the gift of the Holy Spirit, are all there in Holy Scripture; and there are no mightier acts of God than these. My distrust of the phrase is only because it suggests that these mighty acts of God are never to be seen anywhere else. And a real concern in our study of Holy Scripture in education for mission is precisely that we shall learn to see the evidences of the mighty acts of God outside Holy Scripture. We shall read Holy Scripture for the sake of the clues it offers to understanding God's action in the wider theatres of world history.

One would study Isaiah, for example, not merely in order to understand the significance of the Assyrians, or the consequences of monotheism when applied to a specific historical situation. One would also understand that the study of Isaiah and the Assyrians and God would be an essential preparation for understanding Chinese communism and God. How does God use "hired razors"? How does one identify the razors? In education for mission, the study of much of Holy Scripture is bound to have for its purpose the establishment of a position for Christians, from which it will be easier for them to understand what God is now doing in our history. So it would be equally with every great act of God. Our aim in biblical study would be to learn and remember the test of divine action—in creation, in judgment, in guidance, in redemption, in sanctification, in continuing, authentic revelation.

Scripture and Tradition

Together with Holy Scripture, all that can be legitimately named as Christian tradition must be continued. The controlling principle here must surely be that expressed by the Consultation on Church Union at their meeting in Oberlin. "By tradition we understand the whole life of the Church, ever guided and nourished by the Holy Spirit, and expressed in its worship, witness, way of life, and its order. As such, tradition includes both the act of delivery by which the Good News is made known and transmitted from one generation to another as well as the teaching and practice handed on from one generation to another . . . in such sense, the Christian tradition antedated the formation of the New Testament canon. The New Testament canon appears not as separate from or opposed to the Christian tradition but rather as an expression of it. Certainly it is the case that in the Church, scripture and tradition are found together."

The Consultation went on to describe three relationships between scripture and tradition (understood as the whole life of the Church) which deserve consideration. "(1) Scripture is itself included in the tradition. The reading of and listening to the scriptures in worship and the authority of the scripture over the teaching of the Church are essential in the life of the Church. (2) The scriptures are intepreted in the light of the tradition. The Church does not set itself above the scripture; but the Church reads and listens to the scriptures as a community of faith. (3) The scriptures are the supreme guardian and expression of the tradition. This is what the Church intends by its acknowledgment of a canon of scriptures."

Doubtless the last word will never be spoken concerning the uneasy frontier between scripture and tradition in the life of the Church. What is of immediate consequence is the continuity of tradition with scripture, in our education for mission. Believing that the Church is guided and nourished by the Holy Spirit, we are then taught as we reflect on how the Church has been led to frame itself and its teaching and witness in obedience to the divine mission.

One does not need to presuppose infallibility in the tradition. It stands always under the judgment of holy scripture. It stands also under the daily judgment of God in history. The presupposition would rather be that there is nothing which is true in the Church's life which is not, however imperfectly, a response to the divine mission. When the development of Christian doctrine is studied primarily as the Church's response (in terms of the mind) to what God was doing in contemporary history, that study will become an essential ingredient of education for mission. The Church may not have been right in its reading of contemporary history. Its response may have been faulty, one-sided, self-centered. Certainly the confessional responses of the divided Church are intrinsically of far less significance—in terms of substantive theology—than the massive united statements of the early centuries. But as education for mission, the fragmentary response of a part of the Body, caught in the tumult of its own history, may be revealing indeed.

I may not stop to develop all this. All I mean to say is that any true study of the Church—its doctrine, its morphology, its worship, its ministry—is best undertaken from the viewpoint of mission. How did the Church identify God's action? How did it respond? How did it shape itself and its weapons so that it could fight its way through history to where God was at work, and make Him known, and make common cause with Him? These are the questions for the study of tradition, I am sure.

God's Action in Our Time

The second objective of education for mission, I would say, is our training in how to discern God's action in our own time. I find myself using a very humdrum illustration here—that of the Church's search for the right question for planning. Planning is no rare and recondite activity in the Church's life. It goes on all the time, notably without much self-consciousness or preparation, and we generally start, at whatever level, with a kindergarten question, "What would be good for the Church?" This has a certain healthy existential flavor, and it enlists at least some immediate interest. But since we don't even know what the Church is, almost inevitably we have to fall back on its sociological description; we cannot say what would be good for the Church, but we can say what would be good for the little religious club we belong to; and before we are done, our planning is hopelessly untrue to ourselves and to the Gospel—it *is* in fact planning for the Episcopalian club.

Something much like this happens when we ask a second (and more useful) question, What would be good for our society? If it weren't for our ignorance and our sin, this would be a very useful question. Even granted ignorance and sin, it is still useful. But in the end we run up against the same horizon as with the first question; and we are driven back one more step to the only question which Christians really can ask.

That question is, What is God doing? This is the only possible question for planning. It is the only possible question for mission. And education for mission must center on precisely this question and how it is to be answered. Granted all there is to be learned from our study of scripture and tradition, we do not come to grips with our problem until we come to the point of our own commitment. The answer that we shall make as individuals—the answer that the Church corporately will make—is literally a matter of life and death. And we cannot come to those decisions trusting in our preconceptions. The Church must be a listening church. Far more, it must be a hearing church, able and eager to take account of every clue, wherever found, to God's action in our history.

Inescapably, therefore, the major part of our education for mission is likely to take place in the "secular" sphere. Sometimes Christians in our generation are almost heard to speak as if the secular world had some miraculous revelation of God denied to the Church. I do not want to seem to say that. I have lived long enough to have profound reverence for the truth and virtue so often displayed by non-believers, in contrast to the failures Christians must confess. But "social scientist is Pope writ large" to far too many of my contemporaries; and my Protestantism overcomes me at this point.

What is at stake is not infallibility. What is at stake is the absolute necessity for Christians to master every technique for discovering truth. Only so can there be any true education for mission. Whatever man learns about the discovery of truth, and the relentless demands it makes, is a cornerstone of Christian education. Better than anyone else, he knows the consequences of revelation, and the absolute necessity of fidelity to it. Whatever the secularist may think of the educational process, to the Christian it is irrevocably sacramental, and central to the whole process of divine revelation; and it can only be shared fully by those who bring to it the response of reverence and faith.

Response

The third, equally important element in education for mission is surely that of our education in *response*. I call this "education" rather than merely "training," although the latter is clearly part of the matter. If the heart of education for mission is to learn how to identify the divine action in history, then there is necessarily carried with this an equal responsibility that we shall learn how to respond to God's action in faithful obedience. This would certainly mean training in the narrower matters of the techniques of Christian living. It would also mean the deeper questions of the techniques not only of self-knowledge and discipline, but also those which would aid us in the steady examination of the structure of our institutions and our corporate life as Christians, in order that through those structures we might the better obey, and with greater freedom.

Let me discuss each of those in a little greater detail, as much as space permits. Nothing is clearer, to my way of thinking, than the need all Christians in our times feel for a radical new understanding of the life of prayer. I am not at all sure that the great themes of prayer ever change. Intercession, penitence, adoration, thanksgiving . . . these and the like remain the timeless pillars of prayer in any age. It is rather with the forms and disciplines that we are disquieted. We are uneasy at what seems to us excessive individualism, for example—yet we are also vividly aware of the individuality within the corporate whole of humanity which must remain, if prayer is to be anything more than a weary sigh. Nothing is more characteristic of our time than precisely this restlessness as to the relationship of the individual and the whole. Here is an area where we need much guidance from the great teachers of prayer.

Again, there are few who are satisfied with any present scheme of self-examination. If our obedience to mission is to be the central theme of our life, we are not helped very much by simply picking at ourselves against the background of the Decalogue or the traditional seven sins. Here again, one has the feeling that we must be on the threshold of a time of fresh and more searching thought about all this, if we are to keep abreast of our theology with our prayers.

So one could continue, looking at the wide area of so-called "personal religion." And these same thoughts, of course, are voiced with equal power with respect to our corporate, liturgical worship. One has only to read the formative studies of liturgy of the past few years, to catch a sense of the urgency of this task.

On the other side of the picture, "Mutual Responsibility and Interdependence in the Body of Christ" has directed our attention with great power to the examination of our structures, our priorities, our programs, and our communications—all against the background of our obedience to mission. It is at this level that we come to grips, for the first time, with mutual responsibility itself; and such study of structures and priorities is a far more subtle exercise than is sometimes taken to be.

Perhaps because we are in a restless mood, we are likely to keep tinkering with our structures pretty steadily. But the tinkering is often done without any very deep reference to the actual structures of society, or the far more basic theological structure within which we live. All too often, we are concerned primarily with administrative efficiency, or our public image, or the practical necessities involved in our staying as we are, where we are. The kind of information and the kind of rigorous thinking required of us if we are to move forward in organization and structure is still largely an unmapped country.

For example, it is easy for us in the Episcopal Church to look at our antiquated General Convention, and point out obvious modifications and amendments which are needed to keep it going. But we do not often enough look at our General Convention against the background of the metropolitan and regional structures within which we also live, the ecumenical configurations of our fellow Christians, or the actual areas and levels at which the major decisions are in fact made. Even an improved General Convention could be nothing more than an antiquated impediment, calculated to preserve an illusion, and get in the way of obedience. I do not say that this is so, of course. But unless there are other ingredients stirred into the mixture of our study, these dangers remain acute. Therefore any education for mission must include the most searching and relentless use of every skill of social science, calculated to help us to reach the objective view of ourselves which we urgently need.

Equally would this be so when it came to the question of our priorities. To refer again to the Mutual Responsibility document, nothing is clearer than the sentimental way in which its third proposal can be treated. The examples used in that document, of the "new organ" or the "inherited institutions," are of course nothing more than vivid illustrations, to make a point clear. The section does not help us to deal with instances where a new organ may be a very important part of our obedience to mission, or where an inherited institution justly requires massive support and renewal.

All I am saying is that the question of priorities is a very sophisticated question. It cannot be answered at the top of one's mind. Therefore for any Christian concerned with obedience to mission, training in the establishment of priorities, using again the most rigorous instruments we can devise, is a necessity.

Equally would this be so with the proposal that we test all we do by "the test of mission and of service." The broad intention is clear enough. Yet the best service the Church can give to a particular society, in obedience to what God is doing, may not at all resemble what that society superficially understands "service" to mean. The unpopular witnesses, the unfashionable services, indeed many of the "irrelevances" of the Church—often enough these turn out, in the end, to have been the best service the Church could have made.

How are we to be trained and educated so as to be able to make sensible judgments about this? Surely there is no cheap answer. The very establishment of the nature of the Church itself, and of the possible services it can render, is an agenda of the most profound cost and depth.

Finally, again in the phraseology of the Mutual Responsibility document, we must be helped to look with fresh eyes and kindled imaginations at the problem of communication. All too often, the word signifies no more than image-building. It may be, and often is, stretched to include the exchange of information. In some cases, we will use the word, and implement it in practical ways, so that we in fact are talking about our need to interpret one to another, to effect a new level of mutual understanding.

How seldom do we reach the fourth level suggested in the context of that proposal in Mutual Responsibility—the "deep and deliberate involvement" with one another! Yet surely nothing less than this can be the horizon of communication. If it is not destined to become a way in which people and cultures and churches discover their interdependence and their involvement in the single mission of God, then communication is nothing more than a servant of selfishness.

These examples I have mentioned are, of course, from an Anglican document. But I do not flatter myself that there is any special insight in the Anglican Communion on these matters. These are the common problems of all Christians, and I believe common elements in any scheme of education for mission.

14

NATIONAL CHURCH AND DIOCESAN ROLES IN EDUCATION

BY *Carman St. John Hunter*

NATIONAL Church and diocesan departments of Christian education are, in general, made up both of full-time professional staff and elected volunteers. Together, members and staff are responsible for thinking, planning, and working in behalf of those leaders, teachers, parents, and clergy who serve on the educational frontier of the Church in face to face teaching and learning situations. Department members have a supporting role in relation to all those who lead study and action groups, teach classes, direct camping programs, serve in parish and preparatory schools, and work with organizations or informal associations through which persons of all ages and backgrounds are challenged and prepared to take their part in Christian ministry and mission in the world.

The National Department of Christian Education has eleven elected or appointed members and thirty professional staff. While the ultimate focus of the national department's work is the same as that for diocesan departments, namely, leaders and teachers in parishes and those for whom they are responsible, the work of the national department is chiefly carried on through the diocesan departments at home and overseas. The national department plans and executes training programs in cooperation with diocesan leaders, assists in the development of diocesan educational strategy, and prepares written resources for the Church's educational ministry.

The number of elected or appointed members serving on diocesan departments varies from as few as eight to as many as forty. Often these members are divided into divisions within the department each carrying assigned responsibility for different age levels, for diocesan camps and conferences, for leadership training. Sometimes diocesan departments also have divisions for the Sunday Church school, for parish day schools, and for college work. The educational secretary of the Episcopal Churchwomen is, in most dioceses, a member of the adult division of the department. Just over half of the dioceses have at least one full-time staff person who serves in an executive capacity, guaranteeing continuity and responsible leadership for the programs planned by the department members. In eleven dioceses there are multiple staffs of two or more persons who give full-time service in the field of education. No two dioceses are exactly alike and the movement in the last few years has been toward even greater diversification.

A major problem exists in dioceses where geographical distances are great and churches and missions widely scattered, since these are often the dioceses without full-time staff and with the smallest budgets. The volunteer department members, already overburdened with their own parish responsibilities, face enormous difficulties as they attempt to address themselves to diocesan problems. Of necessity they meet infrequently. The absence of any central authority and responsibility for carrying out effective educational strategy leaves them with a sense of frustration. Good plans are often abandoned or forgotten and members feel their time and work have been wasted. Department members frequently have multiple assignments which include other diocesan departments and committees. The many programs seem to be in competition with one another, and fragmentation results. The miracle is that they accomplish as much as they do against such great odds.

The New World

While departments of education have long struggled with problems of planning, execution, and the integration of work into a diocesan strategy, the realities of human existence in a rapidly changing society place these concerns and frustrations in an entirely new perspective. In earlier eras departments were chiefly preoccupied with Sunday Church schools, youth groups, and adult classes as means to increasing individual loyalty to and participation in the Church's own life. It now seems as though many long-forming revolutions have burst upon the Church, shattering earlier images of tasks and functions. Today departments of education more often state their goals in relation to the demand for Christian presence and participation in the world where God is at work redeeming, reconciling, and healing than upon institutional structures for education. It is not that they consider Sunday or weekday education, adult study, and all of the traditional forms of Christian education unimportant. Rather they see the inextricable relation between these and the whole life of people in God's whole world. The questions to which many departments of education are addressing themselves have become:

With what equipment does the Church send men, women, young persons, children into the social, scientific, economic, psychological, political revolutions of the present?

What must be the nature and scope of a Christian education which enables persons to discern the meaning of the present through the eyes of faith? How can Christians become deeply enough grounded in their own heritage to discover and serve on the frontiers of God's redemptive activity in the world?

What strength and openness are necessary if Christians are to understand, communicate with, and serve their fellow men?

How can contemporary men, women, youth, and children be trained for distinctive modes of Christian presence and witness in the world?

In the course of struggling with such questions, departments of education are generally led to certain discoveries about the nature of their task:

(1) Department members need to know a great deal about the total experience of the people with whom they work or prepare others to work and about the nature of the society in which the Church exists today. They must be sensitive to and informed about the realities of our urban society as these affect real people in their own church and community.

(2) Serious study and reflection are necessary if there is to be any translation of biblical and systematic

theology into meaningful thought-forms and language for our time.

(3) Traditional diocesan and national structures with their pattern of divided and competing programs and leadership must be replaced by flexible structures permitting a unified approach to research, goal setting, planning, and evaluation.

(4) Clergy, leaders, teachers do not cause and cannot guarantee insight, understanding, change, and growth but they are essential to it. Alive, caring, searching people are the most important instruments in the educational ministry. Therefore, both the national Church and the dioceses have as a fundamental task the preparation of leaders and teachers for sensitive response to God and His world so that they, in turn, may be used in ministry with others. At the same time, traditional training processes are upset. Understandings regarding who teaches and who learns, who gives and who receives, who trains and who is trained are constantly contradicted in the inter-play of people and events making up modern society. Today's teachers and leaders need constant training in learning.

(5) Outside church buildings Christians live and work without denominational distinction. As Episcopalians learn to choose, to risk, to respond, to serve their fellow men and their Lord in His world, they do so in the company of other Christians. To conduct classes and training events, to plan and study in isolated denominational enclaves is both ridiculous and ineffective. Departments need to work with educational leaders of all Christian bodies in their area, planning together for action which reveals the ecumenical nature of the Church.

(6) The most effective training for involvement in society and community issues may well be given by secular groups and agencies. The Church's educational role would seem to be to encourage participation in training programs and action and to include opportunities for reflection on the meaning of such training and action in groups called together by the Church.

(7) A contemporary scientist has observed humorously: "If it works, it is outmoded." Christian education departments are coming to see that the demands of the new society require not merely new programs but constantly fresh forms of education. To support persons for participation in change means to create flexible, dispensable modes of teaching and learning appropriate to diverse and demanding situations. It means much discarding and reshaping as events and conditions raise questions for the Christian in society.

New Directions

The factors and forces for change here listed have affected departments of education in different ways. One of the most dramatic illustrations of new direction has been the increasing number of dioceses attempting to unify diocesan planning and program development. The creation of the new post of program director in at least eleven dioceses symbolized growing impatience with the fractured, competitive demands of uncoordinated units within the diocesan structure. Just as present re-examination of the function and responsibility of Executive Council departments involves the national department of education in new working relationships with other departments, so diocesan departments of education have been discovering new functions and relationships within the life of dioceses where program departments have been created.

It would be disastrous to assume, however, that reorganization alone can bring into being the kind of Christian education necessary today. There can be cooperative, unified planning for an anachronism just as well as for imaginative, joyous response to the new world. Unless all of the pressures and opportunities hinted at in the list above are taken seriously and together, the Church cannot mobilize for change.

Let us examine briefly some of the elements which might go into diocesan planning in the new world.

1. *Gathering the Facts:* Diocesan leaders without respect to departmental labels or assignments, would make a serious effort to discover what life is really like in the space age, on the planet earth, in international nuclear society, in urban America, in the context of its *own* geographic, cultural, political, social community. Research, data-gathering, studies of all sorts and from all sources would be taken seriously in an effort to get as clear a picture as possible of the real situation of the real people for whom this particular part of the Church bears responsibility. Parishes would be involved in offering information regarding their own needs and concerns, and these would be studied in relation to one another. Informal questioning of persons in and out of the Church regarding the way life is, how they feel, where they see themselves, what demands and joys are real for them would be added to the information coming through more formal and formidable channels.

The New Testament is replete with examples of teaching and learning in the context of concrete human situations. No diocesan planning (or any other planning for that matter) can take place without the collection and analysis of facts. Data concerning the specific events and issues affecting people must be current and accurate. Inter-related issues such as the explosion of scientific-technological knowledge, poverty and affluence, the civil rights revolution, changing standards of behavior, urbanization and mobility, impersonal power structures, standards of education, changing roles of men and women, loneliness, alienation, anxiety, all have their specific local manifestations and are themselves the location and occasions for exposure to the meaning of the Gospel. They must be known, analyzed, responded to by diocesan planners if the Church is to be a force in society and in the lives of people and not a haven from the confusions, joys, and agonies of God's world.

The facts expose the real problems which people have in hearing and responding to the Gospel. When the problems which need clarification and definition are identified in this process, they become the foundation both for long-range and immediate attention in a diocesan strategy.

2. *Determining Goals:* The next step would be for diocesan leaders to make a disciplined, honest effort to state goals and objectives for the diocese consonant with their findings. (Where diocesan boundaries are falsely divisive, joint consideration of a larger region would have to take place, perhaps involving more than one diocese in the planning.) Goals or objectives would be stated along the whole continuum between tomorrow and the twenty-first century. Under such a plan, what the diocese hopes to accomplish in relation to the needs and situations being revealed would be developed by the Bishop and others, representing different skills and interests, experience, and responsibility. Without departmental labels, parish clergy, diocesan staff, lay persons from a variety of vocations would attempt to say where the Church in that diocese should speak, teach, train, lead, in mission and service. They see the Church thirty

years hence and what they can do in the immediate future.

Mutual agreement among the diocesan leaders regarding both the analysis of the situation and the statement of common hope and vision would have to be worked on and differences among the leaders understood and faced as honestly and accurately as possible in the process. One of the causes of competition and fracturing of diocesan program efforts is the untalked-through differences of opinion, not merely the lack of a unified structure. Diocesan leadership must become a team before commitment to a program can occur. Change implies controversy. Too often our Church programs only pretend to have change and real renewal as their objective. We have conferences or write papers *about* issues but we do not undertake to act in relation to the issues or to change attitudes and behavior. We thus keep the fearful happy but we fail to face and to use creatively controversy and conflict. Among diocesan leaders frank appraisal of differences and facing of hard issues can be the means of developing plans for action leading to real reshaping of the diocese and the renewal of its people. The same is obviously true regarding the work of the national departments and the leadership of the Executive Council.

3. *Developing Work Plans:* With the long-range future in the mind, diocesan leaders would focus their attention on immediate objectives of first priority. They would need to make a beginning at assessing the resources available to them and at dividing the work to be done into manageable projects. Decisions would be made regarding the time-span for each project. Persons would be assigned to tasks where their skill and professional training would be most useful.

It is at this point that we can begin to see the value of a unified work strategy for a diocese in contrast to the older, autonomous departmental plan of work. Diocesan capability for response would be greatly increased since real problem-solving would determine structures, and temporary teams would replace the static, long-term, generalized assignments.

4. *Carrying Out the Plan of Work:* Each group of persons responsible for a particular task would have to continue the process of defining the objectives for the tasks and discovering the necessary available resources for its accomplishment. The redefining of specific objectives would need to occupy a good bit of the time of the group during the early stages of planning its task. It is an unfortunate fact that in most Church programs insufficient time is spent in stating objectives. We might well take a clue from the U.S. Department of Agriculture, whose Division of Extension, Research, and Training has pointed the way for many educators:

> People, both individually and in groups, respond best to specific objectives that they believe are achievable. If educational programs are intended to stimulate people to participate, dynamic and achievable objectives are requisite. Such objectives also serve well as the basis for identifying evidence of accomplishment for purposes of evaluation.[1]

The work group would need to be clear about the people to be involved in the project. They would need to state whether the desired outcome is to gain new understanding or to develop specific skills; *i.e.,* what kind of change of behavior is desired. In the development of the work plan, the next step would be to determine the kind of learning experience most appropriate in view of the people to be involved, the resources available, and the kind of change desired. The time schedule for this particular project would be filled in in detail and the step by step procedures for carrying out the project would be identified.

Two On-Going Processes

Two on-going processes are involved, as follows.

(A) *Evaluation:* In both the larger, over-all strategy development and in carrying out of each of the pieces of work assigned to task groups, an unremitting process of evaluation would be essential. Too often evaluation consists of *ex post facto* attempts to discover whether or not those participating in any program liked it or not. Actually, planners need to build evaluation into every phase of program development. From the very beginning stage of gathering data, the planners would need to consider the question of whether or not their methods of data gathering were comprehensive and whether they had really devised means of discovering both the social and personal issues most significantly bearing upon life in their own diocese. Their question might be: Have we arranged for a plan for data gathering that has promise of providing the widest possible picture of the situation in our diocese, in the parishes, and in the composite life of persons in this community?

As goals are determined they must be evaluated in terms of their clarity, explicitness, and the degree to which all those who will have a share in carrying them out will also contribute to their development. The goals of each piece of work assigned to a group will need to be checked in relation to total diocesan strategy. Do they contribute to the realization of the priority goals for the diocese as a whole?

As the design for learning or action emerges it may be evaluated as to the suitability of the learning tasks to the desired outcome. If leaders are to be trained, for example, the educational methodology must include more than a lecture on group leadership, it should make it possible for the learners to have a chance to practice the skills of planning

and leading groups. If, on the other hand, the project involves mobilizing the community for action in changing
housing legislation, then evaluation of the methodology
would mean scrutinizing the effectiveness of the plan for
reaching the power structures in the community.

When the plan for the project has been carried out, then
it must be evaluated for its effectiveness in bringing about
the kinds of changes stated as its objectives. Unless a disciplined effort is made all along the way to look critically at
each step in the process of planning, it will be almost impossible in the end to discover why, for example, the objectives were not attained or what part of the plan was weak.

The process of evaluation is a science. While it should not
be seen as an end in itself, the effectiveness and helpfulness
of the Church's work could be immeasurably strengthened
by an effort to use tools which reveal strengths and weak-
nesses and thus assist planners at every stage in the process
to bring desired results and actual results closer to each
other.

(B) *Theological study and reflection:* Leaders cannot expect that theological understandings will become real for
people unless they are also constantly submitting themselves to the rigorous discipline of asking questions and
seeking to understand faith anew. The never-ending series
of concrete events in life are but opportunities to see and
know what God is doing in His world today. Those can help
others to know Him who themselves have become clear
about the Gospel in relation to the dynamics of the modern
world. The firm conviction that God has already won the
decisive victory and that amid the battles of this life Christians are called to live in ways that show forth their faith in
His victory is the basis for all our strategies and planning. It
is not sufficient for planners to assume this truth and then
go on to develop ever better programs. They too must strug-

gle over how each component part of what they do actually shows forth the Church's faith that God made this world, that man's hope is in Him and that faithfulness to Him is lived out in a vocation of service to humanity.

The Task Today

The direction of this essay may seem to lead toward the end of national and diocesan departments of Christian education as they were described in the first pages. However, the conviction of this writer is far less iconoclastic than it seems. While the solution may, indeed, be the death of present structures, it is possible that change in understanding of function can lead to processes of renewal even within traditional patterns of organization.

There are clear signs that some diocesan departments of education and the national department are presently engaged in new ways of working. Serious attempts to gather reliable data, to make use of scientific findings, to state clear goals for the educational enterprise, to engage in serious theological studies, to assign persons to tasks according to goals are now taking place. Parallel with these efforts in the field of education, similar changes are occurring within other Church programs. Methods and insights are bound to converge and barriers will be shattered as new responses are shaped. Both in the dioceses and in the national Church, new directions have emerged from broadened, fresh understanding growing out of studies and action related to the urban program and to the civil rights revolution. Even where "traditional" departments continue to operate, their life is changed as they work with others in new ways and respond to insights coming from their colleagues in other areas.

Facing honestly the truth about our society, setting goals

and determining response through program can begin and proceed within somewhat archaic structures, provided people approach the basic questions and decisions with freedom and flexibility. In this manner new, more useful, structures can emerge. The functions for which departments stood will continue to be necessary although their relation to each other may change. Social analysis, position statements, theological discernment, will continue to need supporting, educational services by specialists who understand the learning process.

The major question confronting departments of education as they are today and educators in either national or diocesan structures in the future will be: How seriously and how effectively do we take our responsibility to assist Christians to live as a dispersed minority, witnessing and ministering to God's people in an interdependent world where all the scenery has become unfamiliar and all the challenges new?

Some of these challenges will lead Christian education specialists out of the Sunday schools and into the arena of public education. As C. Ellis Nelson has observed:

> A strategy for the future which takes radical pluralism seriously will have to develop a structure of religious education that is coordinated with general education and a program of adult education that is capable of renewing the life of the church in the world.[2]

While Sunday schools may continue for some time to come, educators must enter upon the search for modes and channels of education more consistent with the realities of pluralistic American society.

Just as Christian educators in national and diocesan departments begin to work with their colleagues in other departments and disciplines, so they will be challenged to move into new ecumenical relationships where "cooperation" will soon become a term of the past and mutual ministries will become the common sign of response to God's mission in the world. The same kind of planning described for diocesan and national departments will need to be undertaken together by all of the Christians in any place in the world. We serve a Lord who has already declared our oneness and interdependence across all the barriers of discipline, department, denomination, culture, race, or class. He calls us to move together into His new world. Wherever we go, He has been there first. He knows the pain of change and of freedom. It is He who invites us to discover new ways of working which will release His people from bondage so that with mind and heart and will they may know and serve Him.

15

THE CHALLENGE OF THE ECUMENICAL MOVEMENT TO CHURCH EDUCATION

BY *Randolph Crump Miller*

WHEN the Chapel of Unity at the Coventry Cathedral was dedicated, Dr. W. A. Visser 't Hooft said, "It is a wonderfully encouraging fact that our role is not to create unity, but to maintain it, to hold on to the *given* unity, to receive it from the Holy Spirit." [1]

The Problem of Our Day

The fact remains that there is a broken unity. We have enough unity to realize that we are divided, and as separated brethren:

> We believe that the unity which is both God's will and his gift to his Church is being made visible as all in each place who are baptized into Jesus Christ and confess him as Lord and Saviour are brought by the Holy Spirit into ONE fully

227

committed fellowship, holding the one apostolic faith, preaching the one Gospel, breaking the one bread, joining in common prayer, and having a corporate life reaching out in witness and service to all and who at the same time are united with the whole Christian fellowship in all places and all ages in such wise that ministry and members are accepted by all, and that all can act and speak together as occasion requires for the tasks to which God calls his people.[2]

This statement from the meeting of the World Council of Churches at New Delhi in 1961 is a brief but rich summary of the objective as we now see it. Rather than point to any kind of superchurch, it stresses that "all in each place," whether it be factory, office, school, congregation, or wider geographical area, shall express their unity in Christ. It means the breaking down of barriers between persons, whether ecclesiastical, racial, class, or national. Within the Church, fellowship, worship, ministry, and membership may be shared by all who are claimed by Christ the Lord.

Education for Ecumenical Loyalty

Cardinal Bea, in his lectures at Harvard University, spoke of the requirements for promoting Christian unity. First, he said, we "must first possess an authentic ecumenical *attitude* and let it penetrate and direct our whole teaching and research." This attitude "consists simply in the fact that we seriously accept the New Testament teaching of baptism and its consequences." There is a family unity of the baptized. We need a unity that includes "not only the invisible union of faith and love, but also . . . the external profession and witness of the same faith, . . . the same sacraments, and at least somehow . . . the same Church ministry and order." [3]

Of course, the problem is that this attitude and this unity

are what do *not* exist. The scandal of our divisions is not even believed by many to be a scandal. Although both the World Council of Churches and the Vatican Council have caught the imagination of some people and have changed the climate in which fellowship and communication are possible, little of this atmosphere is shared at the local level.

The challenge of the ecumenical movement can be seen clearly at this point, for the kind of communication between churches which has been achieved at the top level in the World Council of Churches and to some extent more recently between Protestants and Roman Catholics is now a possibility at the lay level. What Cardinal Bea describes as the ecumenical mentality may be only an expression of good will, but when a person achieves this attitude

> he has a constant vision of the whole of Christianity in the whole world and in all confessions, and shapes his work according to this vision. He respects everyone, listens to all, and considers their problems as his own. From such consideration of all those who are baptized in Christ or who at least believe in him, we become more and more conscious of the problems presented by the wounded condition of a divided Christianity.[4]

Using the Roman Catholic translation of Ephesians 4:15, this means "practicing the truth in love."

This is the background for serious study, but it cannot be presupposed. People come with all kinds of previous prejudices, stereotypes, misinformation, and suspicions. Just because others are different, communication must be achieved across all kinds of barriers.

Yet these is a common ground of doctrinal agreement, of beliefs held in common, and the discovery of this area can assist in establishing a trusting and ecumenical attitude. There is a great treasury of a common Christian heritage shared by all churches, and often the disagreements within parties in a given church are greater than those between denominations. For example, there is probably greater theological variety among the students in a denominational seminary that among those in an ecumenical divinity school such as Yale or Union.

Seeking for common convictions does not mean glossing over differences. But the discovery of what Christians hold in common helps to begin study with some degree of clarity, with increasing appreciation of the other, and with possibilities of common action. The historic creeds are a basis for a common loyalty, even though great freedom of interpretation be permitted. The Revised Standard Version of the Bible, originally an American Protestant ecumenical venture, is now officially accepted by Roman Catholics as well, so that we have a common translation of the Bible. Baptism, as the outburst over Luci Johnson's rebaptism made clear,[5] is a commonly accepted sacrament. Developments are occurring in the understanding and practice of intercommunion.

Part of the strength of the ecumenical movement is that differences are not concealed. The attempt to overcome such differences is "not a search for compromise. Faith must not be confused with politics," [6] as Cardinal Bea reminds us. When differences are made clear, it is possible to overcome the lack of understanding of the other's position. The historical situation giving rise to a doctrine indicates why the emphasis is as it is, and the study of historical controversies shows why some groups hold one-sided views.

The problem of vocabulary provides many unsuspected barriers. There is the variety of technical vocabularies which often seem to speak of the same reality with different words; there is the difficulty of expressing traditional ideas in the language of modern man; and there are the new studies of the logic of religious language which throw light on all current usages. Each aspect of this problem needs to be approached in a different way. Ecumenical dialogue has already done much to clarify the issues of different vocabularies; experiments are continuing in attempts to present the Gospel in modern language; developments in linguistic analysis are beginning to provide the insights needed for clarity, meaning, and verification of words used religiously.[7]

One of the most fruitful forms of ecumenical cooperation is common action as the churches and its members respond to the claim of God upon them. This is visibly evident when clergy, nuns, and laity march together in support of racial equality. It is clear in many other forms of social action, in resolutions and activities by such organizations as the National Council of Churches, and in cooperation in study and research. The World Council of Christian Education and Sunday School Association, the Religious Education Association (which includes Roman Catholics, Orthodox, Protestants, and Jews), and the Division of Christian Education of the National Council of Churches enlist professionals and amateurs, clergy and lay people, in many forms of Christian education. The unity gained in such practical activities opens channels for closer relationships at other levels.

The ecumenical attitude may express itself in many forms of cooperative activity, in mergers between denominations, and in support of ecumenical organizations.

Local Church Life

Bishop Stephen Neill says that there is only one method that works to get ordinary lay people interested in Christian union. This is to say, "Just be willing to assume, for a moment, that we are going to have a united Church in Perth, or Milwaukee, or Singapore, or wherever it may be. Now sit down and work out a constitution for that Church that will really work." [8] Such a program might not provide a blueprint for union, but after a long period of careful study the group would know what the issues are, and probably they would become intelligent and devoted supporters of ecumenical action.

For too long, the great statesmen of Christian unity have made all of the significant advances, and what is needed today is an intelligent group of lay leaders in every congregation who are aware of the problems and promises of the ecumenical vision. When such groups from various Church families can be brought together to face problems, the local congregations will find many things that can be done together.

The New Delhi report stressed the point that our common life in Christ is tested most fully in the local situation, and this is where failure is most often experienced. The challenge is that "Christians ought always to do together everything which conscience does not compel them to do separately." [9] The possibilities seemingly are endless. A program of Christian education may sponsor common Bible study, common lay seminars, common lectures. Where these have been attempted under competent leadership, the results in terms of numbers have been surprisingly large and in terms of quality have been satisfying. Local churches also have come together for common worship, especially on festival or national celebrations. Many churches have cooperated in ministering to new people, to minorities, and to the troubled or needy. Common hospital chaplaincies, prison chaplaincies, and armed forces chaplaincies are taken for granted in many places.

The local church, as an institution, faces ecumenical opportunities such as these. Local churches also can come together through lines of organization in councils of churches, which in some cases are beginning to move from a pan-Protestant to a Catholic-Protestant axis, thus providing an even wider base for ecumenical understanding and action.

The educational program behind institutional ecumenical relations must succeed in relating study to action. Simply to read *The Church Across the Street*[10] in a twelfth grade class can provide information and understanding but not acquaintance. Therefore, ecumenical studies should have a purpose that supports improved relationships and common activities.

The associations of modern secular life provide other opportunities for common activities. Men are brought together in academic, professional, industrial, political, and homemaking associations. As denominational Christians, often they seem to be isolated from the Church and therefore unable to provide any kind of witness through decision-making, behavior, speech, or the like. But in such associations, if the barriers to Christian unity have been cut down, Christians may learn from each other and take common action where necessary. Laymen who come together to share what is common in their faith will be strengthened in their vocational commitment in their occupations.[11] The lay academies in Germany stand as a challenge to churches in other countries at this point, for they bring together men and women with common problems and let them struggle with the issues in their lives against the background of Christian faith.[12]

The World Council of Churches and Its Responsibilities

"The great new fact of our time," as Archbishop William Temple called the ecumenical movement, bore fruit in 1948 with the formation of the World Council of Churches. Except for the Roman Catholic Church, every tradition within Christendom is represented. It is no superchurch, but it is a means of bringing churches together in various forms of unity. It has its educative function in order that members of all churches may know what is going on in the world, but it also has its task forces to study many aspects of world Christianity in today's world.[13]

Study of the World Council of Churches will lead to a more ecumenically oriented theology. Daisuke Kitagawa lists some of the issues that need to be dealt with from an ecumenical perspective and for which leadership is being provided by study task groups in the World Council of Churches. First, he says, there is the "integrity of the secular," by which he means that Christians are learning to take seriously the problems of living in the world as issues for Christians. If God is not a "specialist in religion," perhaps we can begin to see that God's concerns are found in the world in which men live, in their secular occupations. Second, this world is being turned upside down by the revolution in technology and in the ethics of work. Man's power, gained through scientific advances and the use of machines, is greater than ever before, leading both to the possibility of destruction and of creative use of leisure time. If society cannot absorb all of its potential workers, what does this say about the relation of toil to the pay check in tomorrow's world? Thus theology and ethics come together in the face of the technological revolution. Third, the development of an urban culture is something new, to which our rural churches and agrarian theologies are irrelevant. The traditional parish, the voluntaristic congregation near people's homes, and the church in the inner city need radical re-examination.[14]

Such problems are best faced in ecumenical conversations. And there are others. The churches have never come to terms with the place of women in church or world. Women have been emancipated in almost every aspect of life, "practically the only exception being the sacred ministry in the Roman Catholic, Eastern Orthodox and Anglican traditions." [15] In spite of spectacular leadership from the few, the Church has lagged in facing the problems of race relations and ethnic minorities.

An ecumenical study group could face up to the following question:

> What does it mean, empirically, to say that one believes in and belongs to the one, holy, catholic, and apostolic church —the community of saints—in a world-wide, open, dynamic, and secular society, growing both ethno-racially and religio-culturally more pluralistic? [16]

Only in such a way will an ecumenical theology be born, based on conversations between Christians in lay occupations and theologians.

Episcopalians and Union

Bishop Stephen Neill makes a sweeping comment

> that almost all those who have entered into United Churches are agreed that, however great the price that had to be paid, the blessings of union are far more than a compensation for any sacrifice that has had to be made. [17]

Anglicanism, including the Protestant Episcopal Church, has had an ambivalent relation to all movements toward union. The Episcopal Church was one of the last major denominations to join (in 1940) the Federal Council of Churches. Yet it had been instrumental in the gathering at Lausanne in 1925 the first ecumenical Conference on Faith and Order. It has provided ecumenical statesmen of the calibre of William Temple. Yet, with one exception, it has backed out of every consideration of merger with another church. It has had conversations with Presbyterians, Lutherans, Methodists, and most recently with the consultation on church union of six American denominations.[18]

This ambivalence surrounds the one success story, the Church of South India. This is the only union of episcopal and non-episcopal churches. Careful theological study, lengthy consultations, consideration of the views of Church leaders throughout the world, and complex voting procedures involving thirty-two decisions of official church bodies led in 1947 to a new church growing out of Congregational, Presbyterian, Methodist, and Anglican traditions. It is a Church with bishops and a new liturgy but it is open to change in the future. No minister entering the union was re-ordained.

Concerning this new united Church, the Lambeth Conference of 1948 was ambivalent, turning in a majority and a minority report. Even now there is not full union, even though a presbyter of the Church of South India became Bishop of Uganda in 1952, indicating that there was no schism.[19]

In the World Council of Churches and in the National Council of Churches in the U.S.A., Anglicans have consistently provided top leadership. Henry K. Sherrill, when he was Presiding Bishop, was one of the presidents of the World Council of Churches and the president of the National Council of Churches. But lay people have not been involved or informed (and in some cases they have been misinformed, as in the ill-founded charges of communism against both organizations).

As far back as 1948, the bishops at the Lambeth Conference wrote:

Reunion of any part of our Communion with other denominations in its own area must make the resulting Church no
longer simply Anglican, but something more comprehensive.
. . . The Anglican Communion would be merged in a much
larger Communion of National or Regional Churches, in full
communion with one another. . . . [But then came the cau-
tionary note] It would be equally a betrayal of our trust
before God if the Anglican Communion were to allow itself
to be dispersed before its particular work was done.[20]

Ecumenical Witness

The most exciting new movement coming out of ecumenical considerations is the ministry of the laity. This refers to
the *laos* or people of God, who have meeting points in the
secular world which become opportunities for the Church's
witness. The Church gathered for worship and study becomes the Church scattered in the world. But instead of
being scattered as Church, it becomes fragmented and the
individual is isolated.

It is irresponsible to get an individual Christian excited
about his mission and then leave him to be crucified.

The damnable thing about so much of this admirably efficient lay programming is that it is so much concerned with
the duties of the layman in his local church, and so little concerned with his duties in the office and the plant and the
supermarket and the downtown slum.[21]

After considering a series of articles on "What's Ahead for
the Churches?" Kyle Haselden concludes that all of them
are preoccupied with their own internal lives; they withdraw prudentially from the arenas of life. "From all angles
the picture is dismaying." [22] Churches find unity based on
personal congeniality, similarity of taste, and equality of social status.[23]

The ecumenical reformation is the hope for genuine union, a union based on Christian faith and not the accidents of birth. Kyle Haselden puts it clearly:

> Our solidarity as Christians does not spring from the fact that we are washed and made acceptable to each other by the same cultural and racial streams but from the fact that we have a common baptism. Our unity as Christians does not rise from our common tastes but from our common Supper.[24]

Our common baptism is the basis for both unity and ministry. It leads to union in Christ and to service in the world. It is the basis for the ministry of the laity. It is a call to a "style of life"[25] which is supported both by God's grace and by the community of the faithful. This support must be on a wider basis than the local congregation, for

> ecumenical organizations are free to try new techniques and emphases, point out new directions, provide experiences of new techniques and relationships, offer aid and encouragement for those who would break out of outworn patterns, discard what is less effective, and move on to other projects.[26]

The cultural, social, economic, and racial limitations of a neighborhood parish are much less in evidence in a council of churches, and therefore there is this freedom to move toward a "style of life" which can be fruitful. It is no accident that witness against racial discrimination is always more effective when a council of churches, especially on a state or national level, is involved.

Vital Questions

One of the starting points in a local congregation is obviously a study group, and it might begin by facing a number of crucial questions:

1. How can I become an ecumenical Christian? In what way can I promote Christian unity within my sphere of influence?

2. What does the Bible say about the unity of followers of Jesus Christ? What disrupted the unity of Christians in biblical times?

3. What is the real meaning of Church membership? Is baptism, whether of infants or believers, a sufficient basis for membership?

4. How is Church unity hindered by such factors as social, political, cultural, national, and racial elements? How much such mixtures can our Church stand and keep open the channels of communication and relationships?

5. What is the difference between organic and federal union? Is it more important that churches merge into one Church or that they learn to work and share together and accept the ministries and communicants of other bodies?

6. Is there any tension between my loyalty to my own denomination or congregation and my loyalty to the worldwide Church? Should I join a united church in my own village or community or travel a distance to a church of my own denomination?

7. Should I support the union of my denomination with another if I think we will lose something "unique" in our tradition? Is there any way to reconcile episcopal and non-episcopal ministries (as they did in the Church of South India)?

8. How can my Church join with others to support Christian laymen as they carry out their ministry in the secular realm? How can we apply Christian principles to the racial problem, poverty, education, hous-

ing, and the like? How can we make Christian stewardship effective in the world?

9. How can we support unity among the churches and avoid the problems of a monolithic institution? Can we keep our pluralism and have union at the same time? Can we keep diversity and freedom and yet give up our exclusiveness within the Christian community?

10. How can we open ourselves to the new theology and the new reformation? [27] Can we develop a theology for today and tomorrow and still keep the conservatives in our fellowship? [28]

Conclusion

We began with a quotation from Dr. W. A. Visser 't Hooft at the dedication of the Chapel of Unity at Coventry Cathedral. In conclusion, we turn to him again:

We talk and act sometimes as if the problems of Church unity are similar to the problems of political adjustment—of the creation of the common market or the finidng of a formula for co-existence between the East and West. . . . We are not asked to build castles in the air, to think up some unprecedented utopia or some clever new scheme, we are simply asked to help the Church be the Church as it is in the mind of its Lord. The great, the full unity exists as a gift which the Holy Spirit offers us when we are ready to receive it.[29]

NOTES AND ACKNOWLEDGMENTS

Chapter 1

1. Quotations from *Herzog* by Saul Bellow, Viking, 1964.
2. Dietrich Bonhoeffer, *Letters and Papers from Prison,* ed. by Eberhard Bethge, trans. by Reginald H. Fuller, Collins, 1959, p. 122.
3. Bellow, *op. cit.*
4. *Episcopal Churchnews,* October 14, 1956, pp. 25, 40.
5. *Circular* of the G.P.E.S.S.U., 1826, and *Triennial Reports* for 1829 and 1832.
6. See O. S. Michael, *The Sunday School in the Development of the American Church,* Young Churchman Co., 1904.
7. See Clifton H. Brewer, *A History of Religious Education in the Protestant Episcopal Church to 1835,* Yale, 1924, pp. 143ff., and *passim.*
8. H. F. Cope, *The Evolution of the Sunday School,* Eaton and Mains, 1911, p. 106.
9. *Loc. cit.,* p. 19.
10. Dorothy L. Braun, "A Historical Study of the Origins of the Seabury Series of the Protestant Episcopal Church," Ph.D. dissertation, School of Education, New York University, 1960.
11. *Cf.* Division of Curriculum Development Minutes for February 28-March 1, 1951, and October 8, 1951, and *How to Create a Living Educational Program in Your Parish,* mimeographed document prepared by the Division, dated September, 1951.
12. Responsible formulations of the function of education are easy to come by, but see, *e.g.,* Joseph Katz and Nevitt Sanford, "The Curriculum in the Perspective of the Theory of Personality Development," in *The American College* (ed. Sanford), Wiley, 1962, Chapter 11, p. 419, in which the authors discuss the limits of the conceptual orientation of contemporary education and state that curriculum is not a body of knowledge. The crucial and exacting discipline facing the religious educator today is the rigorous task of translating average experience into religious issues and relating them to doctrinal and biblical truths.
13. "Tradition and the Individual Talent," in *Selected Essays,* Harcourt, Brace, 1932, pp. 5f.

241

Chapter 2

1. "Constitutions of the Holy Apostles," in *Basic Writings in Christian Education,* ed. by Kendig Brubaker Cully, Westminster, 1961, pp. 76-80.
2. Clifton H. Brewer, *A History of Religious Education in the Protestant Episcopal Church to 1835,* Yale, 1924, p. 174.
3. David H. Hunter, "The Protestant Episcopal Church," in *The Westminster Dictionary of Christian Education,* ed. by Kendig Brubaker Cully, Westminster, 1963, pp. 524-527.
4. Marc Oraison, *Love or Constraint: Some Psychological Aspects of Religious Education,* Kenedy, 1959, p. 117.
5. Dora P. Chaplin, "The Eucharist and Education," in *The Eucharist and Liturgical Renewal,* Oxford, 1960, p. 62.
6. Martin Thornton, *The Rock and the River,* Morehouse-Barlow, 1965, p. 42. Used by permission.
7. John A. T. Robinson, *Honest to God,* Westminster, 1963, p. 99.

Chapter 3

1. Daniel B. Stevick, *Canon Law: A Handbook,* Seabury, 1965, p. 141.
2. For an interesting discussion of this matter, see *ibid.,* p. 142.
3. See "The Churches Expect a Teaching Ministry" by Gerald E. Knoff, in Nathaniel F. Forsyth, ed., *The Minister and Christian Nurture,* Abingdon, 1957, pp. 19ff.
4. Although women have been admitted to many theological seminaries as B.D. as well as M.R.E. candidates for a long time, it is only within recent years that several Episcopal Church seminaries have revised their admissions policies to make this possible. Episcopal Theological School, Cambridge, Mass., Virginia Theological Seminary, and Church Divinity School of the Pacific are examples of Episcopal Seminaries that now award the B.D. to women. Seabury-Western Theological Seminary grants women access only to the A.M. in the field of Christian education. Windham House, New York City, operated as a residential center for women students under the national Church, has had to have its candidates for Christian education study enroll in Union Theological Seminary or New York Theological Seminary, ecumenically oriented schools.
5. "Why does the Church teach? The Church teaches because it cannot help doing so if it is going to be true to its own foundations in the living gospel. The Church teaches in order that a

full and joyous faith may characterize its present generation and be handed on, by the grace of God, to its future members." (Kendig Brubaker Cully, *The Teaching Church*, United Church Press, 1963, p. 19).

Chapter 5

1. Lewis Bliss Whittemore, *The Church and Secular Education*, Seabury, 1960.
2. Alfred North Whitehead, *Science and the Modern World*, Mentor, 1962, p. 19.
3. Mary Perkins Ryan, *Are Parochial Schools the Answer?* Holt, Rinehart & Winston, 1964.
4. Gilbert Highet, *The Art of Teaching*, Vintage, 1957, p. 32.
5. Diane B. Gertler, *Statistics of Nonpublic Elementary Schools*, U.S. Department of Health, Education and Welfare, 1964.

Chapter 6

1. St. Stephen's Episcopal School, Austin, Texas.
2. Iris V. Cully, *The Dynamics of Christian Education*, Westminster, 1958, pp. 18-19.
3. Lewis Joseph Sherrill, *The Gift of Power*, Macmillan, 1959, pp. 82-83.
4. G. E. Jackson, "Christian Education and Theological Method," in *Theology Today*, Jan., 1961, p. 491.
5. Findley B. Edge, "Shall the Layman Teach Religion?", in *Religious Education*, January-February, 1961, p. 55.
6. Randolph Crump Miller, *The Clue to Christian Education*, Scribner's, 1950, p. 19.
7. George W. Webber, *God's Colony in Man's World*, Abingdon, 1960.
8. Daniel D. Williams, "The Theological Aspect of Christian Education," in *Religious Education*, March-April, 1962, p. 86.
9. Paul H. Vieth, ed., *The Church and Christian Education*, Bethany, for Cooperative Publishing Association, 1947, p. 172.

Chapter 7

1. Thomas J. Wertenbaker, *Princeton, 1746-1896*.
2. Quotation from *New England's First Fruits* (1643), carved over Harvard College gates.
3. Myron F. Wicke, *The Church-Related College*, p. 2.
4. Donald G. Tewksbury, *The Founding of American Colleges and Universities Before the Civil War*, Shoe String, 1932, pp. 32ff.

5. Guy E. Snavely, *The Church and the Four-Year College*, Harper, 1955, p. 187.
6. *Ibid.*, p. 187.
7. Manning M. Patillo and Donald M. Mackenzie, *Eight Hundred Colleges Face the Future*, Danforth Foundation, pp. 11-13.
8. Guy E. Snavely, *op. cit.*, p. 1.
9. Manning M. Patillo and Donald M. Mackenzie, *op. cit.*, p. 34.
10. Statement of Purpose adopted by Foundation for Episcopal Colleges at Geneva, N.Y., Aug. 19, 1964.
11. See the statement by the University Senate in *Bulletin of the University of the South*, Sewanee, 1963-64, pp. 10f.
12. *Bulletin of Trinity College*, Hartford, 1964, p. 86.

Chapter 8

1. Alvin M. Weinberg, "But Is the Teacher Also a Citizen?" in *Science*, August 6, 1965, p. 601.
2. Stratton, "The Penrose Memorial Lecture," in *Proceedings of the American Philosophical Society*, Vol. 108, No. 5, October, 1964, p. 393.
3. Robert C. Wood, "The New Metropolis and the New University," given at the Conference on Higher Education for Urban America, Detroit, Michigan, June, 1964.
4. Quoted in *The New Republic*, July 3, 1965, p. 14.
5. *The New York Times*, September 7, 1965, p. 33.
6. Daniel Bell, "The Disjunction of Culture and Social Structure: Some Notes on the Meaning of Social Reality," in *Daedalus*, Winter, 1965, p. 220.
7. The Forward Movement, 1959.
8. Jones B. Shannon, "College Work: Past, Present, Prognosis," in *The Church Review*, May, 1965. Copies are available from The Church Society for College Work, 17 Dunster Street, Cambridge, Massachusetts, for thirty cents each.
9. William Hamilton, *The New Essence of Christianity*, Association, 1961, p. 31.
10. From *The Christian Community in the Academic World*, a statement approved by the General Committee of the World Student Christian Federation. Copies are available from the Federation's offices at P. O. Box 206, 1211 Geneva 3 Rive, Switzerland, for five cents each.

Chapter 9

1. The Ordinal, *The Book of Common Prayer*, Protestant Episcopal Church, pp. 532-533, and 541-543.

2. Constitution and Canons for the Government of the Protestant Episcopal Church, p. 5.
3. The Ordinal, p. 536.
4. Quoted from the excellent essay by E. R. Hardy in *The Ministry in Historical Perspectives*, ed. by H. Richard Niebuhr and Daniel D. Williams, Harper, 1956.
5. In 1964, there were 571 seminaries, plus 459 "scholasticates and houses of study of the religious orders," according to Monsignor John Tracy Ellis in *Seminary Education in a Time of Change*, ed. by J. M. Lee and C. J. Putz, Fides, 1965. For a sharply critical view of this proliferation of institutions, see the essays by James Michael Lee in the same volume.
6. These are: Episcopal Theological School, Cambridge, Mass., Episcopal Theological Seminary of the Southwest, Austin, Tex., Nashotah House, Nashotah, Wis., Protestant Episcopal Seminary in Virginia, Alexandria, Va., School of Theology of the University of the South, Sewanee, Tenn., Seabury-Western Theological Seminary, Evanston, Ill., General Theological Seminary, New York, N.Y., Berkeley Divinity School, New Haven, Conn., Bexley Hall, Gambier, Ohio, Church Divinity School of the Pacific, Berkeley, Calif., and Philadelphia Divinity School, Philadelphia, Pa.
7. H. Richard Niebuhr and Daniel D. Williams, eds., *The Advancement of Theological Education*, Harper, 1956, p. 67.
8. *E.g.* the essay by Gibson Winter in *The Making of Ministers*, ed. by Keith R. Bridston and Dwight W. Culver, Augsburg, 1964.
9. E. O. James, *The Nature and Function of Priesthood*, Vanguard, 1955, p. 293.
10. The Ordering of Priests, *The Book of Common Prayer*, p. 546.
11. The arguments of the writers of *The Advancement of Theological Education* (*op. cit.*), pp. 217ff., seem to me to settle this issue for this century.
12. *E.g.*, John A. T. Robinson, *Honest to God*, Westminster, 1963, and James A. Pike, *A Time for Christian Candor*, Harper, 1964.
13. *E.g.* E. L. Mascall, *Up and Down in Adria*, Faith, 1963, and O. Fielding Clarke, *For Christ's Sake*, Morehouse-Barlow, 1963.
14. A cartoon in *Stars and Stripes*, the Second World War serviceman's paper, showed a tough-looking soldier looking with obvious disapproval at a passing chaplain. Caption: "I'm tired of his unholier-than-thou attitude."
15. For this idea I am grateful to Martin Thornton, especially for his book *Pastoral Theology: A Reorientation*, S.P.C.K., 1960.
16. St. Augustine, *Christian Doctrine*, Book IV, Chapter 2.
17. Martin Thornton, *op. cit.*, p. 268.

18. Georges Michonneau, *Revolution in a City Parish*, Newman, 1950.
19. Paul Moore, Jr., *The Church Reclaims the City*, Seabury, 1964.

Chapter 10

1. A variety of educational materials, planned specifically to relate teaching and learning to liturgical worship, is published by Associated Parishes, Inc., 116 West Washington Avenue, Madison, Wisconsin. The present writer is indebted to these publications for several insights.

2. The *locus classicus* for this outline of the liturgy is the account by Justin Martyr at the conclusion of his *First Apology* (written in the middle of the second century), which has frequently been translated and printed. For a commentary on this material, see H. Boone Porter, Jr., *The Day of Light*, Seabury, 1960, Chapter VI.

3. The practice in many parishes of habitually treating the Holy Eucharist as a pietistic service at an early hour, without sermon, hymns, or other expressions of corporate activity, is of course a flagrant violation of the letter and the spirit of the Prayer Book.

4. See Massey H. Shepherd, Jr., *Liturgy and Education*, Seabury, 1965, Chapter V.

5. Clergy as well as laity do need edification and instruction. The practice of having the officiating priest sit while the epistoler reads the Epistle indicates that he too is listening and being instructed.

6. See Joseph A. Jungmann, S.J., *Pastoral Liturgy*, Challoner, 1962, part 3, especially Chapter II.

7. A most obvious case in point for Anglicans is the widespread disregard of the rubrics of *The Book of Common Prayer*.

8. I Peter 2:1-10; Revelation 1:6, 5:10; *cf.* Exodus 19:6 and Isaiah 61:6.

9. This Greek word (from which our word *priest* is derived) means literally "elder." It is regularly used in canon law to designate a priest in his capacity as an official of the Church.

10. For a lively presentation of the priest's presidency, see *Priest's Guide to Parish Worship* (American Roman Catholic Liturgical Conference), Helicon, 1964, Chapter II.

11. This term, the ordinary Latin word for priest, emphasizes his role as offerer of sacrifice.

12. Romans 15:16.

13. An outstanding account of the "house church" will be found in John A. T. Robinson's *On Being the Church in the World*, Westminster, 1960, Chapter V.

14. For recent thought and practice on these lines, see *New Forms of Ministry*, ed. by David M. Paton, Edinburgh House for the World Council of Churches, 1965.

Chapter 11

1. Emmanuel G. Mesthene, "Learning to Live With Science," *Saturday Review*, July 17, 1965.
2. Morton and Lucia White, *The Intellectual Versus the City*, Mentor, 1965.
3. *The Book of Common Prayer*, p. 49.
4. *Ephesians* 4:12 (RSV). Comma omitted.
5. See Egbert De Vries, *Man in Rapid Social Change*, SCM, 1961. Chapter VI, "The Human Personality in Ferment."
6. *Ibid.*
7. Arthur J. Vidich and Joseph Bensman, *Small Town in Mass Society*, Doubleday (Anchor Books), 1958.
8. Harvey Cox, *The Secular City*, Macmillan, 1965, p. 4. Also, see Editors of *Fortune*, *The Exploding Metropolis*, Doubleday, 1958.
9. Maurice Merleau-Ponty, *Sens et Non-Sens*, Paris, 1948. The key passage is translated by Harvey Cox, *op. cit.*, p. 5.
10. J. Milton Yinger, *Sociology Looks at Religion*, Macmillan, 1961, p. 22.
11. See Gerhard Lenski, *The Religious Factor: A Sociological Study of Religion's Impact on Politics, Economics and Family Life*, Doubleday, 1961.
12. W. Lloyd Warner, *American Life: Dream and Reality* (revised edition), University of Chicago (Phoenix Books), 1962, Chapter 5. Also, by the same author, with Meeker and Eels, *Social Class in America*, Harper (Torch Book), 1960.
13. There are large and stagnant pockets of "disprivileged" in this country wherein there is but little mobility, horizontal or vertical. See Michael Harrington: *The Other America*, Penguin, 1962. (Hence the concern for the "Appalachia" problem and the Federal anti-poverty program.)
14. See H. Richard Niebuhr, *The Social Sources of Denominationalism*, Shoestring, 1954. Also Will Herberg, *Protestant-Catholic-Jew*, Doubleday, 1955; J. Milton Yinger, *op. cit.*, especially Chapters 2, 3, and 4.
15. For a fascinating discussion of the last, see Paul M. Harrison, *Authority and Power in the Free Church Tradition*, Princeton, 1959.
16. For a penetrating discussion of the mass organization of present-

day society see Kenneth E. Boulding, *The Organizational Revolution*, Harper, 1953.

17. In August, 1965, the Medical Association of New Hampshire reported that there were needed immediately 160 additional physicians, mainly in rural communities.

18. The relatively prosperous State of New Hampshire finances most of its school improvements and operating budget by so-called "sin taxes" (levies on alcoholic beverages, tobacco products, and legalized racetracks including the only, at present, state-operated lottery "sweepstakes").

19. Henry Pratt Fairchild, ed., *Dictionary of Sociology*, Littlefield, Adams, 1964. For a more extended discussion see Robert K. Merton, *Social Theory and Social Structure*, The Free Press, 1949.

20. See James Gustafson, *Treasure in Earthen Vessels*, Harper, 1961.

21. Quoted in *The New Reformation?* by John A. T. Robinson, SCM, 1965, p. 27.

22. *The Book of Common Prayer*, p. 539. See *The Secular City* by Harvey Cox for an exposition of the biblical roots of the secular. The argument is, perhaps, overstated in places, and certainly does not give enough weight to the meaning of "holy," but is on the whole provocative and refreshing.

23. John A. T. Robinson, *op. cit.*, p. 29.

24. Gayraud S. Wilmore, *The Secular Relevance of the Church*, Westminster (paperback in *Christian Perspective on Social Problems* series), 1962, p. 47.

25. *Ibid.*, p. 52.

26. To be a "son" in the household, as understood in the New Testament, is to be a mature person with responsibility and authority.

27. The writer has a more extended discussion of this well-known point in *The People of God*, Seabury, 1963.

28. Daisuke Kitagawa, *The Pastor and the Race Issue*, Seabury, 1965, pp. 13 and 43.

29. See especially John R. Seeley, *et al.*, *Crestwood Heights: A Study of the Culture of Suburban Life*, Basic Books, 1956; Sam B. Warner, Jr., *Streetcar Suburbs*, Harvard, 1962, Gibson Winter, *The Suburban Captivity of the Churches*, Doubleday, 1961.

30. See Kenneth B. Clark, "Education in the Ghetto," in *Christianity and Crisis*, Vol. XXV, No. 8, May 17, 1965. Much of the argument would apply *pari passu* to Church schools whose habitat is the "WASP" ghettos of this country.

Chapter 12

1. John Macquarrie, "Christianity and Other Faiths," Union Seminary Quarterly, Vol. XX, #1 (November 1964).

2. Aldous Huxley, *The Perennial Philosophy*, Harper, 1945, *passim*.
3. W. T. Stace, *Time and Eternity*, Princeton, 1952, p. 5 *et passim*.
4. A. N. Whitehead, *Religion in the Making*, Macmillan, 1926, *passim*.
5. F. S. C. Northrop, *The Meeting of East and West*, Macmillan, 1946, *passim*.
6. W. E. Hocking, *The Meaning of God in Human Experience*, Yale, 1912, *passim; The Coming World Civilization*, Harper, 1956, *passim*.
7. Arnold Toynbee, *An Historian's Approach to Religion*, Oxford, 1956, p. 264 *et passim; Christianity Among the Religions*, Scribner's, 1957, *passim; Civilization on Trial*, Oxford, 1948, *passim*.

Chapter 14

1. J. Neil Randabaugh, *Evaluation in Extension*. Division of Extension and Research Training, U.S. Department of Agriculture, 1965, p. 18.
2. C. Ellis Nelson, *Innovations for Church Education*, an unpublished paper, copyright by the author, November 15, 1965.

Chapter 15

1. H. C. N. Williams, ed., *A Vision of Duty: Sermons Preached in Coventry Cathedral*, Hodder and Stoughton, 1963, p. 94.
2. W. A. Visser 't Hooft, ed., *New Delhi Speaks about Christian Witness, Service, Unity*, Association Press (Reflection Book), 1962, pp. 92-93.
3. Samuel H. Miller and G. Ernest Wright, eds., *Ecumenical Dialogue at Harvard: The Roman Catholic-Protestant Colloquiam*, The Belknap Press of Harvard, 1964, p. 30.
4. *Ibid.*, p. 31.
5. See Vernard Eller, "Another Catholic in the White House," in *The Christian Century*, August 18, 1965, pp. 1009-1010; Visser 't Hooft, *op. cit.*, pp. 111-113.
6. Samuel H. Miller and G. Ernest Wright, eds., *op. cit.*, p. 33.
7. See Ian T. Ramsey, *Religious Language*, SCM Press, 1957, and Macmillan, paperback, 1963; Donald Evans, *The Logic of Self-Involvement*, SCM Press, 1963; Frederick Ferre, *Language, Logic and God*, Eyre and Spottiswoode, 1962, and Harper & Row, 1962; William T. Blackmore, *The Problem of Religious Knowledge*, Prentice-Hall (Spectrum paperback), 1963.
8. Stephen Neill, ed., *Twentieth Century Christianity*, Doubleday

250   THE EPISCOPAL CHURCH AND EDUCATION

(Dolphin paperback), revised American edition, 1963, p. 359 (English edition, William Collins, 1961, p. 373).

9. Visser 't Hooft, *op. cit.*, p. 104.
10. See Reginald D. Manwell and Sophia Lyon Fahs, *The Church Across the Street*, Beacon, revised edition, 1962; Louis Cassells, *What's the Difference? A Comparison of the Faiths Men Live By*, Doubleday, 1965; Kyle Haselden and Martin E. Marty, eds., *What's Ahead for the Churches?* Sheed & Ward, 1964; Gustave Weigel, *Churches in North America*, Helicon, 1961 (Schocken paperback, 1965), a Roman Catholic view; Stephen Neill, *Anglicanism*, Penguin, second edition, 1960.
11. Visser 't Hooft, *op. cit.*, p. 105.
12. See Lee J. Gable, *Church and World Encounter*, United Church Press, 1964; Franklin H. Littell, *The German Phoenix*, Doubleday, 1960.
13. See Randolph Crump Miller, *Christian Nurture and the Church*, Scribner's, 1961, pp. 164-182; also Hans Heinrich Wolf, "The Ecumenical Movement," in Stephen Neill, ed., *Twentieth Century Christianity*, Doubleday (Dolphin paperback), pp. 361-398; Ruth Rouse and Stephen Neill, eds., *History of the Ecumenical Movement*, 1517-1948, SPCK, 1954, a thorough coverage of the subject.
14. See Daisuke Kitagawa, "Toward an Ecumenical Theology of Mission and Ministry," in *Protestant Churches and Reform Today*, William J. Wolf, ed., Seabury, 1964, pp. 12-18.
15. *Ibid.*, p. 18.
16. *Ibid.*, p. 20.
17. Stephen Neill, *Twentieth Century Christianity*, Doubleday (Dolphin paperback), p. 332.
18. See George L. Hunt and Paul A. Crow, Jr., eds., *Where We Are in Church Union*, Association (Reflection book), 1965, a report on six denominations. The Anglican Church of Canada has entered negotiations toward unity with the United Church of Canada. The Church of England has been in conversations with the Church of Scotland, the Methodist Church in England, and the Dutch Reformed Church.
19. See Stephen Neill, *Twentieth Century Christianity*, pp. 134-136.
20. *Lambeth Conference, 1948*, SPCK, 1948, Part I, pp. 22-23. See F. P. Coleman, "Ecumenism in the Anglican Communion," in *Ecumenism and Religious Education*, Loyola, 1965, pp. 44-57.
21. Mark Gibbs and T. Ralph Morton, *God's Frozen People*, Westminster, 1965, p. 181. See Pierre Berton, *The Comfortable Pew*, Lippincott, 1965, for a view of Anglicanism in Canada.
22. Kyle Haselden and Martin E. Marty, eds., *op. cit.*, p. 203.

23. *Ibid.*, p. 213.
24. *Ibid.*
25. See Francis Ayres, *The Ministry of the Laity*, Westminster, 1962, for a description of a Christian "style of life."
26. Report of the Department of Ecumenical Education of the Cleveland Area Church Federation, December 1964, mimeographed.
27. See John A. T. Robinson, *The New Reformation?*, Westminster, 1965; Harvey Cox, *The Secular City*, Macmillan, 1965; Gibson Winter, *The New Creation as Metropolis*, Macmillan, 1963; James A. Pike, *A Time for Christian Candor*, Harper & Row, 1964; and of course John A. T. Robinson, *Honest to God*, Westminster, 1963, and David L. Edwards, ed., *The Honest to God Debate*, Westminster, 1963.
28. These questions are modified from J. Robert Nelson, *Overcoming Christian Divisions*, Association (Reflection Book), 1962, pp. 117-126.
29. H. C. N. Williams, *op. cit.*, pp. 94-95. Every book mentioned in these notes could be the basis for lay study of the significance of the ecumenical movement.

INDEX